Dreaming Your way to
Creative Freedom

Other Books by Lucy Daniels

Dreaming Your Way to Creative Freedom

✦

A Two-Mirror Liberation Process

Lucy Daniels

iUniverse, Inc.

New York Lincoln Shanghai

Dreaming Your Way to Creative Freedom
A Two-Mirror Liberation Process

iUniverse books may be ordered through booksellers or by contacting:

iUniverse
2021 Pine Lake Road, Suite 100
Lincoln, NE 68512
www.iuniverse.com
1-800-Authors (1-800-288-4677)

ISBN: 0-595-34393-7

Printed in the United States of America

To everyone who seeks more freedom and power in themselves
and in their creative work.

Contents

Acknowledgments

I want to acknowledge with warmest gratitude two people without whom this book would never have seen the light of day—Holly Peppe and Mary Lee. In addition, many thanks go to Susan Toplikar and her students at North Carolina State University's College of Design and the many artists, musicians, dancers, and writers who have participated in my seminar on creativity: all have helped me appreciate how what I've learned could be valuable to others.

I'm also grateful to Jeff Dale for the imaginative cover art that brings my dream images to life.

Preface

This book is the result of my own successful struggle to overcome a decades-long writer's block. It is also an in-depth analysis of what artists do all the time—use their mistakes—and what teachers and psychotherapists repeatedly advise—"learn from your mistakes." What distinguishes my approach is where I look for errors and how I put these discoveries to use.

By simultaneously attending to problems in my writing and to the content and evolution of my dreams, I came to see how my unconscious _required_ the very shortcomings in my work that I was laboring to correct. Further study also enabled me to learn about my personal unconscious symbolism, knowledge which made my dreams even more intelligible and helpful. I now call this my two-mirror liberation process, and in the pages ahead I will show you how to employ it for yourself.

Though the material in this book is predominantly my own, experience in conducting seminars with a mix of creative people, including artists, writers, musicians, opera singers, dancers and choreographers, has led me to see this reflective process as having universal potential. In my own life, as in the lives of some clients seen in my clinical psychology practice, this approach has helped resolve life problems as well as creativity problems. While each inner journey provides its own unique adventure highlighted by an individual's personal unconscious symbolism, the route for each traveler is essentially the same. I offer this book as a map for you to carry on your own freedom-seeking journey.

Dreaming Your Way to Creative Freedom

Free vs. "Blocked" Creativity

"Freedom is nothing left to lose," Kris Kristopherson sang in the 1970's. Therefore, even when it is deliberately sought, freedom involves the pain of loss and can be hard to tolerate. Creating individuals, whose aim it is to continually put new things into the world, encounter this dilemma more than others.

My experience as both a once-blocked writer and a psychologist involved with a variety of creative individuals has led me to conclude that truly "alive" creating has to do with transforming and projecting one's innermost feelings and beliefs outward into a work of art that reflects them not only to the world but also back to the self. Therefore, since we can only produce what we can bear, it is essential that the creator be able to accept both the truth being expressed and its form. Furthermore, creating transforms very personal material into symbolic form that may hide the "true" meaning from its creator until it's out there to be observed "objectively" but also, sometimes with surprising distress. Depending on your life history, this distress may be mild, non-existent or severe. Some may be spared distress altogether by having the unconscious capacity to wait or unconsciously prepare to undertake a project that might otherwise be threatening.

In my view, we cannot explain creativity, but we can often identify, understand, and remove its "blocks." When I say this, however, I am using a personal, slightly different definition of "block." Whereas writer's or artist's block is typically thought of as a psychological conflict that *stops* creating, my broader definition includes any *unconscious* conflict that interferes with an individual's capacity to create effectively or to accept what he or she produces. The unconscious plays a central role here. Since conscious wishes and intentions may be the exact opposite of unconscious ones, the unconscious can mess up conscious ways of representing things.

The simplest way to explain how these unconscious problems interfere with creating is to say that they undermine the freedom and authenticity of our

1

human capacity to symbolize. Symbolization's crucial role in creativity has been cited by several psychoanalytic writers, but psychoanalyst Susan Deri wrote about this most extensively. She studied symbolization in her treatments of creative individuals and wrote an entire book on the subject, which I will discuss later. (1)

Our different life experiences leave each of us with a unique set of personal unconscious symbols. I found mine in dreams while undergoing psychoanalysis and have learned over the years from both patients and seminar participants that other dreamers can, too. By carefully examining and thinking about the content of our dreams, we can also learn how our particular symbolism may be hampered by unconscious beliefs. This knowledge is invaluable, because, again simply put, we cannot create what we unconsciously cannot bear. Our unrecognized illogical beliefs won't let us. And since truly alive creating advances us to ever more daunting levels of freedom, even very successful artists can expect to continually run into difficulties. This book is dedicated to resolving such problems through what I call "dreaming your way to creative freedom."

The Two-Mirror Approach

Dreaming your way to creative freedom is not as easy as it sounds. But it *is* possible if you can be patient and are willing to focus on your self, your creative products, your life history (and the personal symbolism developed through it), and your dreams. I call this process the "two-mirror approach" because it entails seeing yourself in both your creative work and your dreams and using the insight possible with logical reflection on these revelations to make freer choices.

In my case this process was enhanced by the combination of psychoanalysis and persistent efforts to return to writing. I will describe this later. While your journey may also be enhanced or accelerated by psychodynamic treatment, you can, like many others I've known, gain considerable creative strength using this approach without treatment.

If you're motivated, the two-mirror approach I outline and illustrate in this book should pay off generously. Armed with awareness of specific weaknesses in your creative work and with knowledge acquired from your dreams about what unconscious beliefs require your ineffectiveness, you will be freer to do otherwise. Here's what you'll need to do to make the process work for you:

1. Write a detailed story line of your life with careful attention to objects, feelings, people, settings, and issues dominant at different periods. Include a detailed description of your current psychological situation.

2.　Gradually develop the habit of realistically and critically appraising your creative work, striving to be honest and precise about its strengths and weaknesses. In doing this, keep it in mind that flaws and process problems *can* be keys to freedom. This work appraisal should become a daily enterprise. When you notice a specific problem in either your products or your process, you need to take time out to write it down to think about later.

3.　Record your dreams immediately upon waking and before you think about them. Be sure to record their dates as well.

4.　Over time, pay attention to the images in your dreams with particular focus on recurring and/or slightly changing images. Similarly, note the settings of your dreams and the ways you appear in them. Keep a record of these symbols and settings as you go along. This will help you recognize your own unique unconscious symbols and the meanings of their variations.

5.　Continue this process, as outlined above, to become more and more proficient at utilizing these two mirrors: your creative work with its strengths and weaknesses and your dreams' portrayal of the unconscious basis of these conditions.

6.　Be patient. You will need time and experience to become familiar enough with your personal symbolizations to be capable of powerful insight into the workings of your own psyche.

The first step in using my own dreams as orienting mirrors was discovering my personal unconscious symbols and gradually developing skill in recognizing and using the information they provided. Indeed, the fact that initial puzzlement and contemplation led to thrilling understanding of why I appeared in some odd guise in a particular dream made me realize how very much my dreams knew about me that I was oblivious to consciously! Then little by little I realized how much this knowledge based on my past experience could benefit my endeavors in the present. In my personal symbolization, for instance (which will be explained more fully in the dream journey portion of this book), urination represents the act of writing; shoe type represents the quality of that writing product as I currently experienced it; the room my father wrote in after World War II represents my unconsciously remaining in my father's writing space rather than claiming my own. Also, since I actually do write by hand on a yellow pad, hands in different forms in my dreams are symbols that show the changes in my unconscious view of my writing process.

As I continued to work at writing armed with this growing awareness of my personal symbolism, I gradually developed what I now refer to as a "mountain-climbing grapple" approach to utilizing dreams and dream images. This approach embellishes J.B. Pontalis' concept of dreams as transitional objects ("comforters" that ease transition from the old and familiar to the new and unfamiliar) and utilizes dream images in a more active pursuit of freedom. It involves seeing what is "wrong" in the picture and focusing consciously on how to make the dream image "right" through making changes in your creative work and life. For instance, as you will see from my dream examples, I responded to a dream image of my writing hand in a cast by setting aside one bedroom in my house as a writing room. With this intense self-examination and questioning, I became devoted to conflict resolution and ego defense revision, seeing how I "protected" myself from dreaded-as-painful awareness and then worked to accept the lesser temporary pain of effective truth.

Since dream images are much closer to life's ambiguity and complexity than our conscious concepts of conflicts and defenses can be, such "dream climbing" is continually surprising and often liberating. Now, I also use a "back-grappling" approach to compare dream images recorded years apart that nevertheless contain significant similarities and differences. With ego strength, insight, and life accomplishments increasing in the course of analysis or through accumulating dream and self knowledge, "back-grappling" permits me to see new things in old dreams. Both these techniques have enabled me to better understand my unconscious conflicts and to actively use this increased knowledge of the unconscious to consciously pursue greater capability.

And this effort quite naturally led to yet another tremendously helpful discovery, a "two-mirror approach" to the pursuit of emotional freedom. Developing this approach prompted me to rename the series of seminars I've taught for the last ten years for people involved in a variety of creative endeavors. The new name, "Our Problems As The Roots of Our Power," refers to how observing shortcomings in our creative work can make us aware of how the work we produce is not as effective as we need it to be. Focusing on these shortcomings can enable us to be specific about the problem. If you simultaneously dream and can focus on the manifest dream and the unconscious truth it reveals, you have the opportunity both to understand how a particular unconscious conflict necessitates ineffective creative expression and to consider whether to remain confined by this conflict as well as what you may have to do and face to overcome it.

Yet another benefit of this dual mirror approach is the continual parade of new discoveries it can add to one's problem-solving arsenal. Some that I routinely rely on include:

a. Staying on the lookout for new guises worn or new self-images in dreams and becoming more skilled at understanding their meanings.

b. Learning the symbols used and coming to understand why you have these particular ones.

c. Remembering that "bad" dreams often serve the function of restoring the fear or low self-esteem one's unconscious regards as the "norm" and therefore, requires to feel "stable."

d. Staying alert to word play as well as to visual images. For instance, how a rabbit can mean "hair."

e. Similarly remembering that a "good" dream may come as a "reward" for an actual failure to grow.

f. Remembering that "anxiety dreams" serve the double function of reminding us that something in current life is anxiety-provoking and allowing us to feel that all this distress is "just a dream."

g. Always asking, "Why *this* dream at *this* time?"

h. Always responding to the place and time of a particular dream with the questions, "How was I feeling and/or doing in that place/time?" or "What was happening to me then/there?"

In addition to my own experience, I've had the advantage of learning from the participants of the 18-week seminar I've taught for the past twelve years. These seminars have included writers, visual artists, musicians, opera singers, choreographers, and advanced students at the North Carolina State University College of Design. Some who took my first seminar ten years ago are still meeting monthly in their homes to share their dreams and their creative products and processes. Not only do these individuals now regularly consult their dreams for information needed to do their work; their creative products also reflect use of group discussion and dreams, *and* their dreams reflect responses to changes in their work.

I'm an ever more devoted user of the two-mirror process, and this book is yet another outgrowth of that devotion. In it I show the continued usage of my own dream process in relation to creative work produced during the same period. As I present my journey in a nearly thirty-year psychoanalysis in pursuit of ever-increasing freedom to write, my hope is that others will be able to utilize this process—in treatment or not—to achieve their personal freedom and creative goals.

As the book itself will demonstrate, my work with dreams focuses on the manifest dream (the straight-forward recalled experience) and on trying to recognize and understand my personal symbols. It also relates these to the problems in my writing and employs the "mountain-climbing grapple" approach to actively put this dream knowledge to work. This perspective does not depend on just the "correct" interpretation. Each individual's understanding is most meaningful for that person alone. While input from others (therapist, fellow creator, or bystander) is always valuable, in this enterprise no authority outranks the self. This includes, of course, being free to recognize mistakes as opportunities to learn about yourself. Although others may be able to see us as we cannot see ourselves, no one can have the copious, in-depth self-knowledge accumulated in each individual.

But more on that later. For the moment, welcome to my freedom quest, which will begin, as I did myself, with exploration of the rich literature produced by dream experts over the last century. I will summarize relevant highlights of this for you here, beginning with the ubiquitous Sigmund Freud. I also offer a bibliography of dream and creativity texts for those who want to know more.

Beginning with Freud

In 1899, Sigmund Freud declared "...Dreams are the royal road to the unconscious." He then went ahead with his major contribution—*The Interpretation of Dreams*—to present psychoanalysis and his understanding of neuroses, using dreams and the dream process as demonstrations. While Freud's work was groundbreaking and valuable, it has contributed more to the psychoanalytic perspective about and treatment of neuroses than to major understanding of dreams. In a sense, *The Interpretation of Dreams* was a book ahead of its time, because understanding the unconscious and the mind's conflicts with itself was needed before the dream could be done justice.

Freud's perspective on dreams reflects his brilliant deciphering of psychopathology. He viewed forbidden unconscious wishes stirred by the day's perceptions and experiences as the basis for dreams. He held that the actual expression of such forbidden wishes was likely to be altered in a dream in order to partially satisfy the dreamer without disrupting sleep. He also focused on three main elements to be considered in dream interpretation: *the latent dream* or the (often forbidden) wish that is seeking fulfillment; *the manifest dream*, which is what the dreamer consciously experiences and reports; and *the dream work* or defense mechanisms which translate the latent dream (wish) into the manifest dream. The intricacy of the dream work distortions as they protect the sleeper from true awareness (just as symptoms do the neurotic) is a major facet of Freud's dream theory.

Though Freud, like the rest of us, was limited by his time, many of the discoveries made during his preparation of *The Interpretation of Dreams* laid the foundation for the much greater understanding of dreams we have today. In the second half of the twentieth century, other psychoanalysts, benefiting from Freud's skilled and in-depth descriptions of neurosis and intrapsychic functioning, have provided useful new understanding of dreams. These newer perspectives involve attributing importance to other psychological factors in addition to the drives and defenses that were Freud's focus. These more current interests include the significance of "objects" ("psychoanalyticese" for the usually human object of such drives as need, anger or love), the "self" (self-esteem and identity issues), and "affects" ("psychoanalyticese" for emotions) as well as the drives (impulses) that Freud considered paramount. Yet another approach, initiated later in Freud's lifetime, views dreams as having central psychological functions such as relieving emotions and problem solving. Ego psychology, which began with Freud, Anna Freud and Heinz Hartmann in the 1920's, takes this position.

Unlike Freud, later ego psychologists focused on the manifest dream instead of the dreamer's wish and the dream work. Erik Erikson expressed this perspective in explicit detail in his landmark paper, "The Dream Specimen of Psychoanalysis" (1954). Erikson states that what the dreamer needs to attend to on awakening is the manifest dream and the information it can impart. Though, like Freud, he considers the dream directly related to both the unconscious and the events of daily life, Erikson's emphasis is on the observable details and the sequence of images in the manifest dream.

Hanna Segal, another early ego psychologist, carried Erikson's point of view to greater depths. In "The Function of Dreams" (1981), Segal discusses the complexity of symbol formation required in dreaming. She points out that individuals differ widely in ego strength and, therefore, in the capacity to dream effectively (so that the needed psychological work is accomplished). In her view, individuals who have not achieved the capacity to deal with and accept loss and separation lack the ego strength needed for fully effective dreaming. Therefore, she says, when such individuals dream about upsetting material, their dreams are concrete and explicit rather than symbolic. The function of such dreams, she says, is either to dump unbearable feelings or to predict their being acted out.

Two examples of her theory are: an angry or paranoid dreamer dreaming about a tantrum and a continually procrastinating dreamer dreaming about being late (and later actually being late). In general, Segal emphasizes the form and function of dreams as opposed to their content.

The knowledge accumulated from the mix of theoretical perspectives applied to dreams in the last sixty years has benefited me tremendously in my pursuit of emotional and creative freedom. The focus on symbolism initiated by Segal has been particularly useful because of its emphasis on the concrete.

Symbolization—Its Function and Afflictions

The significance attributed to symbolization in dreams and other mentations and behaviors increased as psychoanalysts began emphasizing the function of the ego (the reality-mediating facet of the psyche). Freud had not disregarded symbols; he had simply focused on their roots (wishes and defenses) rather than on symbols themselves. Moreover, his scheme of the human psyche and its interacting components provides us with a basis for understanding what is involved in the uniquely human capacity to symbolize. The bare essentials of the human psyche in Freud's system (which I am grossly simplifying here for the sake of practicality) are as follows:

> *The conscious* is the psyche's peripheral component that receives information from the external world as well as from the body and the mind. It is characterized by logical thought (also called "secondary process") in verbal language form.

> *The unconscious* is composed of mental contents and activities that are not logical ("primary process") and are representative of the instincts. Some contents have never been conscious due to rigid censorship; other unconscious contents were once conscious but were then repressed due to feeling unbearable. In the unconscious, opposite instinctual impulses (such as love and hate, fear and desire) can exist side by side without affecting each other. The pleasure principle (acting on impulse to relieve tension) and timelessness predominate.

> *The preconscious* is intermediate between the conscious and the unconscious. Its contents may be considered unconscious descriptively, but they are readily accessible to consciousness. In contrast to the formless mobile energy of the unconscious, the energy of the preconscious is said to be "bound." That is, it has form or is imaged as in images, dreams, sounds, concepts (cold, small, strong, and so forth) and *symbols*. Although the preconscious may be influ-

enced by the primary process of the unconscious, it tends to operate, like the conscious, with secondary process and logical thought. Freud assigned various functions to the preconscious that we now associate with the ego: conscious memory, making choices to inhibit or discharge feelings, and intrapsychic communication of feelings and ideas.

Other Freudian psychic components useful in considering symbolization and dreams are *ego*, *id* and *superego*. *The ego* is the problem-solving aspect of the psyche. It contains conscious and unconscious mechanisms as it mediates between internal and external reality. *The id* encompasses mental representations of the instinctual drives and some but not all of the unconscious. The id contains everything inherited. With psychic development, the id can evolve into the ego. *The superego* sets up and maintains an intricate system of ideals, values and rules. It is largely unconscious and often at odds with both id and ego.

As I hope is evident from the delineation above, the preconscious is the psychic component predominantly responsible for symbolization, dreaming, and creating. We are fortunate that analysts who came after Freud have been able to utilize his work in gaining understanding of the symbolization process and the problems that can compromise it.

Symbolization and Creating

Susan Deri, an Hungarian-born psychoanalyst who emigrated to the U.S. in 1940, saw the basis of creativity as our human capacity to symbolize and thus create something new that bridges a gap. Deri's book, *Symbolization and Creativity* (1984), sets forth her theory, beginning with the view that the separation or lack supplied by a gap is essential, but not sufficient, for creating to take place. Hope and time are also necessary. As Deri puts it, "Without hope, without trust in the future, there can be no creativity." One intriguing thing about Deri's emphasis on the human capacity to symbolize is that it applies in all kinds of situations where distance or separation is a factor: the separateness of child and mother, between lovers or friends, between an artist's or writer's feelings and an appreciative audience, between a problem in the world and a scientist's idea, between an individual's conscious and unconscious, or between external reality and individual perception.

Deri believed that individuals differ in their creative ability and that this determines the degree to which emotional problems can undermine the creative process, with geniuses succeeding despite problems. For Deri (in contrast with Karl Jung), our symbols are individually based and bridge separations between the self and the other, as well as between an individual's conscious and unconscious. Symbol formation is a directed process that organizes experience. Personal symbols and images are ways we represent certain aspects of life to ourselves. While there may be some similarities (type of car or house frequently represents the dreamer), each individual's symbols and images are unique.

Thus, for Deri, problems in creativity are problems with symbolization, and she views the unconscious as the culprit in these problems just as Freud would. Or more specifically, repression, which forces material back into the unconscious, is the demon. In considering the problems repression causes with symbolization, it helps to focus on the identifying and active qualities of the symbol. As Deri tells us, a symbol both connects and separates. It deals with an absence. It allows expression, but expression that is neither immediate nor the raw feeling itself. Missymbolization (which can occur in a variety of forms) distorts these necessary characteristics of symbols.

Deri defines the most frequent forms of missymbolization as follows:

> **Desymbolization**: Since the preconscious form of a memory, feeling, wish, idea and the psychic form of its content are wiped out, there is no way this material can be expressed to oneself or to others. (No expression at all.)

> **Cryptosymbols**: Due to partial or total repression, material is expressed in a way that hides rather than conveys meaning. (Ineffective creative product; neurotic symptoms such as phobias or psychosomatic illness that conceal the true problem.)

> **Protosymbolism** is the effect when the gap is missing. Then symbols become *signs*. When there is no separation between what is represented and its representer, the same material is repeated unimaginatively. (Temper tantrum for anger; same story repeated over and over with little variation in fiction.)

While Deri focuses on creativity, it is important to remember that these same missymbolization problems can plague dreams and other communications with one's self and others. In contrast with these problems is the ***presentational symbol***, Deri's term for a well-articulated work of art. This occurs, she says, when there is open and repeated communication between the creator and the work. That results in "a complexly interwoven unity of thoughts, feelings and imagery. Its meaning is not built up in a linear fashion from separate definable elements but has to be grasped in a simultaneous perception of the whole." (1, p. 173)

Lawrence Kubie (1896–1973) was an American psychoanalyst, teacher, and researcher whose contributions focused on understanding how neurotic and psychotic mechanisms undermine psychological freedom by compromising the symbolic process. He considered recognition of the role of the central nervous system essential to such psychoanalytic understanding. This included seeing that with disease or trauma the body, in defense, can become its own enemy. Kubie concluded that when the symbolic process fails or is interfered with by repression, *the symbolic processes themselves serve to perpetuate and fixate the emotional distortions*. What happens when such interference takes place, he said, is that the distorted behavior, symptoms, and compromised symbolism are insatiably and obligatorily repeated because of being repressed. Thus neurotic behavior—especially, for us, unsuccessful expressive symbolism in our creative work—is continually repeated because the goal at which it aims is never achieved.

Kubie placed great emphasis on conscious awareness and was always in dogged pursuit of the truth. Consciousness is freedom in his view. As he put it, "The man who is normal in the psychoanalytic sense can accept the guidance of reason, reality, and common sense. The outside world may be unyielding; but to the extent an individual remains flexible, modifiable, and educable, he is, in a pragmatic sense, *free*. This, indeed, is the most important freedom of all: freedom from the tyranny of the unconscious." (2) Kubie's explorations carried him outside psychoanalysis into various fields of art and service as well.

Of particular interest here is Kubie's book *Neurotic Distortion of the Creative Process* (1958). In it he, too, sees the key to effective creativity being *the capacity for conscious symbolization*. In this "realistic form" of symbolic thinking, he says, we are clearly aware of the relationship of the symbols to that which we intend to represent. The symbol's function is to communicate the hard core, bare bones of thought and purpose. Kubie sees this as one end of a continuum with the other end being characterized by stereotyped, repetitive, distorted symbolism due to dissociation of the symbol and the root it represents.

As Kubie continues, "In the preconscious use of imaging and allegory many experiences are condensed into a single hieroglyph which expresses in one symbol far more than one can say slowly and precisely, word by word, on the fully conscious level. This is why preconscious mentation is the Seven-League Boot of intuitive creative functions. This is how and why preconscious condensations are used in poetry, humor, the dream, and the symptom." (3) But he adds, "The contribution of preconscious processes to creativity depends upon their freedom in gathering, assembling, comparing, and reshuffling ideas." (4)

For this to happen effectively, there needs to be continuous interplay of preconscious processes with conscious and unconscious processes. As Kubie puts it, "…it is the preconscious type of symbolic function which frees our psychic apparatus (and more specifically our symbolic processes) from rigidity. Where conscious processes predominate at one end of the spectrum, rigidity is imposed by the fact that conscious symbolic functions are anchored by their precise and literal relationships to specific conceptual and perceptual units. Where unconscious processes predominate at the other end of the spectrum there is an even more rigid anchorage, but in this instance to unreality: that is, to those unacceptable conflicts, objects, aims and impulses which have been rendered inaccessible both to conscious introspection and to the corrective influence of experience, and which are represented by their own special symbols in impenetrable and fixed disguises. *As long as their roots remain unconscious, the symbolic representative will remain unmodifiable.* This is what renders them rigid. Yet flexibility of symbolic imagery is essential if the symbolic process is to have that creative potential which is our supreme human trait." (5)

Kubie goes on to confront the dubious or reluctant neurotic artist by saying, "As long as preconscious processes function freely, no scientist and no artist need fear that to sacrifice the unhappy luxury of being neurotic will leave his creative powers paralyzed. Quite the contrary, if he emerges from the tyrannical and rigidly stereotyped domination of his own unconscious processes, his creative potential will be freer both quantitatively and qualitatively. I emphasize this because so many artists, so many writers, and so many scientists as well, are literally terrified of getting well. They have a strange and defensive fear that if they give up their neuroses they will cease to be creative, not realizing that to escape enslavement to their unconscious will free their preconscious creative potential." (6)

Creating As A Transitional Process

Expanding from Kubie and Deri, we encounter more recent and current psychoanalysts whose focus has been personal creativity. Most prominent among these is Donald Winnicott, a British pediatrician who became a psychoanalyst during World War II. Winnicott's view of the transitional process and transitional objects (7)—using familiar objects, activities, feelings, attitudes, etc. to assist with the uncertainty of approaching new things—has been a constant support in my own journey and, now, in my efforts to help others involved in similar struggles. Psychoanalyst and artist Marion Milner, a Winnicott admirer and protégé, also wrote an extremely helpful book about the relation of creative projects and the inner self. Though she does not deal with dreams in *On Not Being Able to Paint* (1957), Milner does relate creative work to the individual's inner self, as I do with the help of dreams.

Psychoanalyst Gilbert Rose also deals specifically with the problems of creating. Like Milner, he sees problems in creative work as the normal expected byproducts of its realness. These creative analysts—Winnicott, Milner, and Rose—introduced me to the "transitional process" in creativity, a process by which writing or painting or any creative endeavor can become a means of discovery and growth for both self-liberation and creativity. Working with this perspective turns blocks and botches into opportunities. It also makes creating a more vital process, because it prompts you to stay "awake" or "aware" all over your body as you work. Why all over your body? Because awareness is something the unconscious works very hard to prevent. Therefore, it comes to us in the least likely ways and at the most unexpected times, and we have to be alert not to miss it. When you stay emotionally alert in this manner, even the most painful negative feelings become just information, shreds of truth that, if used, can help free both the creator and the work from unconscious constraints.

The "transitional process," as you might imagine, is an outgrowth of Winnicott's transitional object or the baby's first "not-me" possession, an object that comes into use near the end of the first year of life and that allows the child to have the illusion of mother's presence when she is absent. Winnicott was explicit that the transitional object is neither the teddy bear or comfort blanket nor the baby's internal feelings that this teddy bear is mother. Rather it's both at once, as it provides a bridge between the familiar (baby and mother) and the disturbingly unfamiliar (the larger world). And the "transitional process" as Gilbert Rose describes it in *The Power of Form* (1980), is one in which "the interplay between separateness and union, originality and tradition gives rise to creative imagination." (8)

More Recent Dream Explorers and Experts

Since the advent of ego psychology, most experts on dreams, regardless of their specialty, have to some degree addressed both symbolization and problem-solving. Besides the unique contribution made by each of these psychoanalysts, together they provide a useful perspective on how our knowledge of dreams has expanded over the years. While I've selected a few especially pertinent examples for illustration here, you can find a more comprehensive list of dream theories and their initiators in the bibliography.

In his book, *Memory in Mind and Brain* (1990), Morton Reiser provides examples of how our life experiences, all the way back to our earliest days, are filed inside us according to the emotions that accompanied them. Therefore, we can learn a great deal about ourselves from the temporal or spatial location of a dream. Among other things, we can know that the situation (time and/or place) revisited in the dream demonstrates the feelings and the unconscious associations connected not only to the dream and any past time or place it depicts, but also to situations we currently face in life.

Erika Fromm and Thomas French were ahead of others in emphasizing the problem-solving function of dreams. In a 1962 paper, "Formation and Evaluation of Hypotheses in Dream Interpretation," they demonstrated how, starting with the classical approach, dreams can be studied as cognitive, integrative attempts of the ego to solve current Here-and-Now conflicts. They refer to these as "focal conflicts" and see them as always relating to one or more infantile conflicts. They also speak of dreams as "artistic products of the thinking, groping mind."

French and Fromm continue:

> The dreamer uses simultaneously ideation and more formally organized logical thought in producing the dream, just like the poet, the composer, and the painter do in their creative activities. And dreams, when once fully understood, are fascinating works of beauty.
>
> In order to understand a dream, the interpreter must involve himself open-mindedly in a parallel re-creative, non-schematic process. It is an intuitive activity. But if it is to be more than a hit-or-miss spouting off it requires also scientific self-discipline and the willingness to evaluate critically and conscientiously the ideas and hypotheses one has arrived at intuitively. (9)

About twelve years into my writing-dreaming journey, I discovered the valuable perspective of J. B. Pontalis in *Frontiers in Psychoanalysis: Between the Dream and Psychic Pain* (1977). Essentially, Pontalis views dreams as transitional objects—that is, experiences that allow us to move with less distress into new and unfamiliar psychological spaces because we carry old and familiar material with us. One extension of this Pontalis perspective is that dreams are structured to feel psychologically like the body of the mother. As a result, they allow the dreamer to consider mildly disturbing unconscious material with enough comforting support so that he/she does not have to wake up and thus can continue sleeping and dreaming.

Other theorists have contributed still more enlightening discoveries about the problem-solving capacities of dreams. According to them, not only does such problem-solving allow the resolution of problems that *cannot* be solved consciously, but dreams are routinely used to maintain the self state most familiar to the unconscious or to alter self-esteem so that we can return to this state. Joseph Weiss provides graphic examples of these functions in "Dreams and Their Various Purposes" (1986). This paper includes accounts from a study by Dr. Paul Balson of the benefits of dreams as reported by prisoners of war. Sometimes these were warning dreams that put a soldier on guard; sometimes they were dreams about home or loved ones that comforted prisoners as nothing else could have. Weiss concludes this paper with a particularly poignant example of the power of dreams to provide solutions not possible any other way:

> "The dreamer, a 30-year-old carpenter who was the father of two children, came to therapy after he killed his wife in a shooting accident while unloading a defective gun. The shooting was truly an accident, and the patient's wife died instantly. The patient, at the beginning of his treatment (which was not an analysis), was distraught and indeed suicidal. He felt intense grief and guilt. His therapist focused on the accidental nature of the killing and in various ways supported the patient in his struggle not to think of himself as a murderer. After 8 months of therapy, the patient attained enough relief of guilt to permit himself to produce the following vivid, realistic dream: "I accidentally shot my wife. She staggered to where I was sitting, then lay dying in my arms. As she was dying, she told me that she knew that my shooting her was accidental, and she forgave me for it."
>
> The patient was able in this dream to offer himself much-needed relief and consolation. He kept the dream in mind for a long period of time. He reacted to the dream as though to a real event—that is, as though his wife had in fact forgiven him. He was relieved by the dream despite the fact that he knew it was only a dream and that his wife was dead and could not forgive him.

"This dream makes apparent the power of dreams, with their vividness and closeness to experience, to carry a message to the dreamer. The patient could not offer himself comparable relief by simply telling himself, 'My wife would surely forgive me.' This dream, like the blissful dreams of captured soldiers, offered a desperate dreamer an experience he could remember and use to console himself for a long time after he produced it." (10, pp. 234)

Robert Stolorow and George Atwood in "Dreams and the Subjective World" (11) set forth their interest in "structures of experience" as they apply to dreams. Specifically, they address how symbolization in dreams is heavily influenced by the individual's need to maintain the organization of experience. Thus they see dreams as "guardians of psychological structure" that fulfill this function through concrete symbolization. They give examples of two different ways this works. According to the first, dream symbols actualize a particular current organization of experience in a dramatized and vivid way that reinforces it. In the second, dream symbols serve to restore a subjective world threatened with disintegration. Both cases emphasize the role of dream symbolization in maintaining psychological integrity.

Mark Solms, in his application of both neurological and psychoanalytic understanding to his study of dreams, has demonstrated the incredible complexity of the dreaming process. As Solms shows in "New Findings On the Neurological Organization of Dreaming: Implications for Psychoanalysis" (12), this complexity makes dreaming similar to many other behaviors in terms of the number of different brain areas involved. It also demonstrates a neurological basis for many of the significant unconscious characteristics Freud ascribed to dreams.

James Fosshage is a prime spokesman on the subject of dreams as problem-solving mechanisms. In "The Psychological Function of Dreams: A Revised Psychoanalytic Perspective" (1983), he writes:

> "The supraordinate function of dreams is the development, maintenance (regulation), and, when necessary, restoration of psychic processes, structure, and organization…Dreams attempt to integrate and organize current cognitive-affective experiences through the development and consolidation of new structures, the maintenance of current structures, and conflict resolution. The dual purpose in dreaming, as with all mental activity, is the maintenance of current structure while concurrently moving progressively toward more complex levels of organization." (13)

All these writers and their work have been valuable guides in my own effort to find the emotional freedom to write the way I need to. Besides their specific contributions of knowledge, these writers have helped me feel supported and less alone as I made the advances and personal changes required by my journey. In addition, the work I was determined to produce, and labored to actualize, presented new opportunities to learn and, as a result, provided new tools for my freedom-seeking arsenal. My belief is that readers who pursue their own creative-freedom marches will experience similar exhilarating success.

End Notes

1. Susan Deri, *Symbolization and Creativity* (International Universities Press, Inc.: New York, 1984).

2. Lawrence S. Kubie, *Practical and Theoretical Aspects of Psychoanalysis,* (New York, 1950) 16-17.

3. Lawrence S. Kubie, *Neurotic Distortion of the Creative Process* (University of Kansas Press, 1958) 34-35.

4. Ibid, 37.

5. Ibid, 37-38.

6. Ibid, 38-39.

7. Donald Winnicott, *Playing and Reality* (Tavistock Publications: London, 1971) 1-25.

8. Gilbert Rose, *The Power of Form—A Psychoanalytic Approach to Aesthetic Form* (International Universities Press, Inc.: New York, 1980) 111.

9. Thomas French and Erika Fromm, "Formation and Evaluation of Hypothesis in Dream Interpretation," *Essential Papers on Dreams,* ed. Melvin R. Lansky, M.D. (New York University Press: New York, 1992) 183-196.

10. Joseph Weiss, "Dreams and Their Various Purposes," *Essential Papers on Dreams,* ed. Melvin R. Lansky, M.D. (New York University Press: New York, 1992) 213-235.

11. Robert Stolorow and George Atwood, "Dreams and the Subjective World," *Essential Papers on Dreams,* ed. Melvin R. Lansky, M.D. (New York University Press: New York, 1992) 272-294.

12. Mark Solms, "New Findings on the Neurological Organization of Dreaming: Implications for Psychoanalysis," <u>Psychoanalytic Quarterly</u> 64: 1995, 43-67.

13. James Fosshage, "The Psychological Function of Dreams: A Revised Psychoanalytic Perspective," *Essential Papers on Dreams,* ed. Melvin R. Lansky, M.D. (New York University Press: New York, 1992) 249-271.

Dreamer's Life History and Circumstances

Since every individual's life history and experiences are major influences on their work and their personal symbolism, it is imperative that anyone undertaking the method described in this book make a detailed timeline of their life to date. In each life period some unique and profound influences may not be apparent in the timeline even though they are crucial and may later be recognized as such in dreams. My timeline is below. But while my *life* can be read pretty much in chronological order, many of the character-shaping experiences barely mentioned here are described in greater detail which explains their impact in the background notes following some dreams.

March 24, 1934	Born in Durham, North Carolina.
	Eye surgeries and exercises to correct strabismus.
	Early years included much solitary confinement in family's walled garden.
1942	Elementary school and increased independence with family living in Washington, DC during World War II when Jonathan Daniels was press secretary to President Roosevelt.
1946	Onset of Anorexia Nervosa.
	Back in Raleigh, NC with Jonathan Daniels succeeding his father as editor of the News & Observer.
1947	Sent to boarding school (George School in Bucks County, PA).
1949	First published short story (*Seventeen Magazine*).
1950	George School insisted on treatment before any return to school.

18

April 1951	Hospitalized.
November 1955	Left hospital. Took GED.
September 1956	*Caleb, My Son* published by Lippincott.
	Began work as reporter at *Raleigh Times*.
1957	Guggenheim fellow. Married Tom.
1958	Birth of first child, Patrick.
1960	Published articles in *Virginia Quarterly* ("Half a Lavender Ribbon") and *Coronet Magazine* ("Black Out in Prince Edward").
	High on a Hill published by McGraw-Hill.
	Birth of second child, Lucy.
1963	Birth of third child, Jonathan. Decided "I'm not a writer."
1966	Birth of fourth child, Benjamin.
1968	Entered college at North Carolina State University.
1972	Phi Beta Kappa. Earned B.A. in Psychology from University of North Carolina at Chapel Hill.
1974	Marriage ended. Psychoanalysis began.
1976	Divorced.
1977	PhD in Clinical Psychology from UNC-CH.
	Director of Psychological Services for Lee Harnett Mental Health Center in Lee County, NC. Began private practice.
1979	Death of my mother.
1980	Resumed writing.
1981	Death of my father.
1986	Remarried (Rudy).

1989	Sold my share of *News and Observer*. Established Lucy Daniels Foundation (LDF) and Lucy Daniels Center for Early Childhood (LDCEC)
1991	Divorced.
1991–present	Private practice; offering seminars on "Our Problems As the Roots of Our Power" at the LDF; actively working at LDF and LDCEC.
	Writing stories, memoir, novel. Grandmother of 7.
2001	Death of my sister Bibba.
2002	Publication of memoir *With a Woman's Voice—A Writer's Struggle for Emotional Freedom*.
	Sudden death of my psychoanalyst (after seeing him for 27 ½ years) while I continued work on the novel begun in 1997.
2004	Completion of novel, *The Eyes of the Father*.
	Publication of short story, "Virtuoso."

My Dream Journey

The collection of dreams I present here is by no means comprehensive. With less attention to space and time limitations, I could easily have used four times this number of dreams, most of them contributing to significant breakthroughs in my life and work. Instead, in order to let the power of these self-reflectors shine and communicate their amazing truths most vividly, I have chosen to include only about fifty examples from my thirty-year struggle in pursuit of writing freedom. In selecting these examples I've focused on significant junctures (such as distress or breakthrough) in my writing effort and on dreams that clearly reveal useful self-information otherwise unavailable to me. When it did not conflict with these criteria, I've also tried to portray the symbols common in my dreams as well as the development of repetitive patterns in dream material. (In considering interpretations of specific dreams, please remember that "correctness" has not been my aim. Rather, self information—from success or failure—is what most contributes to creative freedom.) In order to allow further clarity about my symbols, the life experiences contributing to them, and the meaning/impact of these for my freedom journey, I've provided background information after some dreams and their aftermaths.

It may also be useful for readers to know that prior to resuming my effort to write while undergoing psychoanalysis, I rarely dreamed. And when I did, it was always the same—I was wandering lost and alone across a barren landscape.

Examples from the Dream Journey

Example #1

<u>August 1982</u>

I was on my first trip to Europe in a relatively new and exciting relationship with the man who would become my second husband four years later. I was also in my seventh year of psychoanalysis. Having completed my doctorate as well as a four-year stint as psychological director for a rural mental health center, I was now able to focus on my practice in Raleigh and my children. I was also beginning to work at the writing my analyst had been asking about for a couple of years. However, this work confronted me with flaws in its style—woodenness and weakness, for instance—which had contributed to my abandoning writing twenty years earlier.

> The setting was an institution. A mental hospital. And I, at once a doctor and a patient, was sitting on a toilet in a bathroom like those on the acute wards with no doors on the cubicles. But the commode was much further off the floor than normal. I was trying to urinate…trying…trying…but couldn't. My name was announced on the loudspeaker. My name, but the wrong one: "Lucy Daniels. Dr. Lucy Daniels, please call 2973." I didn't know the way, but at the nurses' station, the telephone told me that my family doctor was waiting on the chronic ward. To get there I had to go out the locked door of the acute ward and in the locked door of the chronic ward. Also, my clothes were wrong. I was wearing one of the white gowns acute patients wear. I tried to stand behind the window curtain to hide this, but no one seemed to care. And even though I had no keys, everybody else there did and was glad to unlock the door for me. The nurse on the chronic side had a twitching dimple; she nodded as she let me in but did not speak.

<u>Dream Aftermath</u>

This dream surprised me. But I was quickly able to associate the feelings about not being able to urinate and about being back in the mental hospital with my new writing struggle. After that, associating writing with urinating made sense, too, because it reminded me of having needed to urinate outside my parents' writing room in early childhood. I had been required to stay in our walled garden alone most afternoons between the ages of two and five. During those times the need to urinate had confronted me with a terrible dilemma: as a good little girl I would ask to be let inside to use the bathroom, but interrupting my parents to do so always enraged Father. These memories helped me to see that I unconsciously considered writing to be an intimidating throne I'd inherited. At the time of the dream my name was Dr. Lucy Inman; therefore, being called Lucy Daniels, my writing name, might also refer to me as a writer. And trying to get from the acute ward to the chronic ward could be interpreted as trying to move from abstaining from writing to struggling with it. Doing so—writing when I wasn't good at it—could feel even more shameful.

After this, I continued my renewed effort to write with more understanding of my feelings, especially the shame and my lack of any sense of entitlement. This helped me realize that my shame and sense of inadequacy were associated with the emotional issues writing represented for me rather than with just the writing itself. That discovery made it easier to continue writing, but it also alerted me to the task of recognizing and dealing with unconscious conflicts. One means of helping myself do this was keeping journals—those black and white speckled composition books—where I recorded both my dreams and the thoughts and feelings I was trying to come to terms with. I referred to these journals as "my copybook," as I'd called my notebook when I was a reporter. Eventually I began an autobiographical novel.

Example #2

May 1987

Hard work on the autobiographical novel brought me to where I recognized that its point of view was a problem. Focusing on this, I became concerned about how to present the story most directly, with the least amount of excess insulation. As I puzzled over this, I nevertheless felt increasingly hopeful about the book as a whole. And that feeling enabled me to think about my basic conflict—acknowledging the female and sexual aspects of myself vs. staying "safely" unsexual, or like my parents' "boy" in a way that kept my writing boring. (Part of our family's complex secret trauma was my role as replacement son.)

> I was stark naked in the kitchen of a castle and compulsively eating everything in sight. Embarrassed, pushing open the door to go upstairs to eat in private, I was stopped by the whites of two eyes shining at me out of the corridor's darkness. They belonged to a tall slender black man. Scared, I slammed the door to keep him out, only to discover he was already half inside.
> "Please don't look at me," I pleaded, and he complied by turning his head. Next I noticed my old striped bathrobe—the one I've loved as a coat of many colors—dumped in a heap under the table. It was ragged and only held together by pieces of gauze basted inside. Still eating, I struggled to pull it on with my free hand as I said to the black man, "My mother did this patching to keep it from unraveling altogether." Head averted, he helped me.
> …Then I was upstairs alone and *wearing* the robe of many colors. But there was a gaping hole in the wall due to an earthquake. The house was collapsing.

Dream Aftermath

With this dream, I recognized compulsive eating as a defensive way of stuffing myself to get rid of sexual feelings. Also, in the dream, of course, this was because I felt attracted to the male coming in the door. His blackness likely symbolized both my hostility toward him and my fearful need to keep him subordinate. The coat of many colors could convert me to my parents' "boy" (like Joseph's coat identifying him as his father's favorite son) and would therefore also protect me from Father's sexual advances and from being attacked for competing with or surpassing him as a writer. I also recognized the coat of many colors as the way my mother had needed to keep me "remarkable" as a replacement for the son she had been unable to give my father. The earthquake made me see how devastated I would feel if I as a woman and a writer *did* surpass my parents.

Being able to recognize these issues and conflicts allowed me to go on writing. Furthermore, I was able to simultaneously struggle with the point of view question *and* maintain some hope for the novel.

Background:

This dream, like other most helpful ones, brought together symbolizations of important issues from different periods of my life. To cite just a few:

(a) By this time I had married Rudy, who enjoyed gourmet cooking as much as his intellectual accomplishments as a professor. Probably, too, his emotional intensity and mix of warmth and occasional cruelty resembled my father more than I'd consciously realized.

(b) My anorexia conflicts, though managed better, remained strong and clashed with Rudy's devotion to cooking.

(c) In the household of my childhood, having a way with words had clearly been the key to self-worth. Both my father and my grandfather were respected writers and newspaper editors. So, in a family where females were devalued, I early set my heart on becoming a writer, too. But this identity-shaping wish involved complications as well. My father's first wife, also a writer, had died in childbirth bearing a son who also died. As the first of three girls born to my parents, my wish to be a writer further set me up to fill the slots of these important but secret personages from my father's past. Being the writing son had additional power in the present, because only males were eligible to succeed as editor of our family-owned newspaper. Furthermore, my father repeatedly lamented (but did not try to correct) his having had to live his life in the shadow of our grandfather. Therefore, when my mother strained to compensate for her own sense of inferiority by narcissistically praising my achievements, Father responded with jealous ridicule. By adolescence, the largely unconscious conflicts associated with all this had begun to wreak havoc on both my writing and my identity in the form of anorexia nervosa in response to my achievements. At that time, too, Father began brutally attacking me about my refusal to eat. And these attacks were all the more disastrous because I confused Father's declaring, "You are destroying this family" in response to my refusal to eat with my own guilt about publishing my first short story. During that same period Father sometimes (often after attacking me) called me his "lovable boy" while holding me on his lap.

Example #3

April 1989

As my manuscript expanded, the need to be self-observant and even self-critical came to the fore. In working to improve the writing, I learned to study parts that were poor with a sense of relief. Being able to discover what made them ineffective, how that ineffectiveness made me feel, and, sometimes, that that feeling and its fantasy (and, therefore, *that* ineffectiveness) could be given up provided me with a new sense of self-capacity. Once again the three shortcomings that bothered me most were "weak," "shallow," and "wooden." Recalling how these same qualities had stopped me earlier, I felt discouraged. But soon, I had another most helpful dream:

> I was on Dr. H.'s couch, telling him about having drunk 2 ½ glasses of wine. Suddenly I noticed that my right hand was in a cast and, then, that this was responsible for a good feeling all over my body, a kind of white-light goodness that enveloped me. But different from analysis, in the dream I was lying on my left side, looking at the wall beside the couch and turned away from Dr. H.

Dream Aftermath

So there I was feeling good all over due to being a crippled writer! But it took a long time and lots of work to make this identity-shaking image something I could consciously try to overcome. The earlier steps in this process involved seeing that the compulsive goodness I'd had to maintain all my life (despite feeling it was only a cover for the shame and guilt associated with being praised by my mother) was really reaction formation—an unconscious defensive reversal of conscious feelings or, in my case, driven love for parents I also hated, and a way to keep me bad and them good in my world view. I also had little difficulty seeing that my wrist in a cast represented my view of myself as a sexual cripple. Since two-and-a-half glasses of wine was an amount I considered a little too much, I began to think of a "little too much" in many ways (wine, food, work, exercise, too many words) as something I did to keep myself feeling dead or "good!" With that equivalence, I could also see goodness all over my body as a way of feeling like my father's dead first wife whom he'd adored. Needing to be loved by Father might be keeping my writing "perfectly dead" or in a "cast" that preserved me as his small "copy." Seeing these multiple meanings marked the start of a burgeoning capacity to manipulate symbols, an ability that ultimately became my key to freedom.

What followed from this dream and its associations was a lot of analytic work (on my own and in the copybook, as well as with Dr. H.) to shed the reaction formation. My conception of this task took the form of trying to *understand how to remove the cast from my wrist and the white goodness from my body*. It did not take long to see that the cast on my crippled wrist represented anorexia and that the goodness all over my body symbolized the reduction of guilt possible through not eating or writing too much. That made freeing myself and freeing my writing seem synonymous. Equating my boring, too-packed writing problems with the cast and the straitjacket of goodness was not hard either, but again, doing what was required to eliminate these problems seemed daunting.

Example #4

Fall 1989

In the short run, the only tangible result of recognizing this basic conflict (of unconsciously feeling that crippled writing kept me "good") was a decision to set up a writing room where I could leave my work all scattered about. This was especially necessary because I did not like sharing the dark library where my husband wrote. Six months later, after converting a bedroom to my writing room, I had another dream:

> Going back to the Shamrock Drive house where we raised the children, and where I both went back to school and got divorced, I found a team of laborers renovating it. On the second floor, I entered the writing room Father used after the War, a sunny, high room that had been the nursery before we went to Washington. My own black analytic couch was under the window looking west in the same position as my desk is in my writing room now. I lay on it face down, while Father worked at his writing table across the room. Strong sexual feelings in my vagina indicated to me that I had to leave. Standing up to do so, I was weeping. Father turned out to be Dr. H., dressed in the kind of suit Father wore, and a smaller identical copy of Dr. H. was with him. It made me even sadder to see that his boy could stay while I had to leave.

Dream Aftermath

Obviously, being sexually alive was something I associated with having to separate from both Father and Dr. H. Also, my wonderful marriage of three years and now my private writing room seemed concrete evidence of such aliveness. In analysis we'd been talking for a long time about how Father had called me his boy in terms of my being a writer and the replacement for the son he had lost. We'd also talked about my ashamed willingness to regard my intelligence as masculine being both a defense against Father's sexual provocativeness and a way of meshing with his need to keep me his boy—a copy who wrote like but would never surpass him. However, besides conceptualizing the problem of confusing my writing room with Father's, this dream integrated many significant details I never would have been able to consider consciously. For instance, Father's writing room replacing the nursery pictured how my sisters and I had been raised to treat him like a baby, which was another prohibition against competing with him. I got the idea that a struggle would have to ensue between Father and me before I could ever claim my own writing room. But two details did not take on full significance until four years later—that the powerful vaginal feelings were also symbolic of mouth power (having a strong voice) and that, as I was leaving, Dr. H. and his boy were utterly silent.

Working to effect the separations represented in this dream, I understood that pain and grief were inevitable. My ultimate ability to write with power seemed far from certain, but going the extra mile for my own integrity and emotional freedom had by then become a conscious shaper of my life. At this time, I was already in the process of negotiating to sell my share of our family newspaper, a sale that would give me the funds to both provide my children with graduate education and establish the Lucy Daniels Foundation and Center for Early Childhood.

But the grief I had to face came in more than one form. The changes in me resulting from analysis and my work in writing and in life led to both the consciously worked-for separation from my family of origin and the unexpected end of my cherished second marriage after my husband became explosively and implacably enraged. The results of selling my shares of our family newspaper had been foreshadowed in a dream which depicted me as no longer recognized by my family and my writing as frozen but melting. But, as with the terrible pain around the end of my marriage, I had no capacity at that time to anticipate the gratification possible with freedom.

I responded to these losses and the resulting grief by hunkering down to work harder at writing.

Example #5

December 10, 1990

By this time Rudy and I had been separated four months. I had also completed the establishment of the two non-profit organizations that would bear my name. Since all this made me need my writing more than ever, I worked with increased dedication to complete the autobiographical novel. Then, on the birthday of my sister Adelaide, who is twenty months younger than me, I dreamed:

> I was in this dormitory suite with a bunch of other women the morning of exams. My exam was at 3:00, but the others left me alone there long before that. I was sitting in this church pew, facing high-up (light from a skylight) sunshine. Then I realized I'd urinated on my beautiful red dancing skirt. I got up and decided to put a white skirt over it to hide the wet. But standing in front of this tall mirror to see how I looked, I realized that the white one wasn't long enough to cover the red one. Also, that below those skirts I was wearing these high black walking/riding (writing?) boots that were stolid and businesslike looking and ruined the dancing effect of either skirt. By then it was nearly time for my exam. I was worried because I hadn't prepared in the usual way. Because I was already experienced and proficient in the subject matter, I hadn't studied like a "greasy grind" (Father's name for me when I got good grades in school). And that made me anxious even though I'd made a deliberate decision not to. Suddenly I was afraid I had nothing to write with. I got frantic. But in the bathroom drawer, in the packet that used to hold my diaphragm, I found two substantial black pens. Black and plain looking like the riding boots.

Dream Aftermath

Since by then I'd come to consider that Rudy's emotional disintegration had, like Father's attacks in adolescence, resulted from his not being able to tolerate my increasing good fortune, success, and sexual aliveness, I had no trouble seeing how sitting on the worshipping seat messed me up sexually. There I was, still trying to cover up angry, alive, sexual me with saintliness. But fortunately it no longer worked. A new and surprising discovery from this dream was the idea that I felt anxious *because* I was experienced and *not* making "greasy-grind" preparations. Yet, it took some time to realize that the "test" before me then was writing without the protection of feeling inadequate and overworking to compensate. The fact that the two pens in the diaphragm pouch looked staid and substantial like my walking/riding boots added to my wishful writing question about how to trade those boots in for dancing shoes. And the whole business occurring on Adelaide's birthday made me wonder how this test was related to that of her birth. Two possible answers: I remembered having lost my voice (having become hoarse) the day she first arrived home when I was twenty months old. And, when I was still quite small, Father had hurt my feelings while carrying her, saying that I was "big enough to walk." That hurt had been the greater because Adelaide, as a baby, had gleefully participated in Father's raucous sexual games, while I had "hidden" from them in the shadows of furniture. In response, Father had declared me "an intellectual with no feelings and no sexuality."

The analytic work after this dream moved more substantively into how both my parents had, in different ways, forced penises on me. I had exerted tremendous effort to prevent this in earliest childhood, while at the same time straining to be valuable as both the nurse-mother our family needed and the intellectual success expected of boys in our family. In the period following this dream, on the advice of two interested but rejecting agents, I had to reduce the length of the novel from 700 pages to 500. When I discovered a simple way to do this, I developed an itching, burning rash that helped me recognize that my use of excess words was a defensive response to my intense unconscious need for insulation.

Example #6

April 6, 1991

Still at work on the autobiographical novel, I had also begun dating a psychoanalyst. He was a fine person but our times together seemed more work than I thought they should be. I had the sense that if I continued the relationship I might end up again being a dutiful caretaker in a way that would compromise the rest of my life. Because I was genuinely fond of this man, whom I saw as needing a permanent partner, it was hard for me to figure out how to say goodbye. In this context, I dreamed:

> I at puberty (like the pubescent Skipper doll in my office playroom) and another four-year-old little girl doll were both naked as we drove down to do something at the Haizlips' house. I felt so embarrassed by my nakedness that I put on a layer of tissue paper to hide it. But when Tom Haizlip came to the door, I was so embarrassed to be seen like that that I dove down onto the floorboard of the back seat. The naked littler girl had to drive us home.

Dream Aftermath

I recognized both Skipper dolls as representations of me in different phases. The naked prepubescent doll driving the car I imagined being the Oedipal me who, at four, had spoken powerfully to Father about his dead and secret first wife. The pubescent doll wrapped in tissue paper and hiding on the floorboard would be me, gifted and as a "gift" in adolescence because I was afraid for my sexuality to be seen. Probably, too, that tissue paper represented my anorexia. Seeing this enabled me to consider that, among other things, anorexia had been a way to silence my "too strong" voice. The fact that both girls were dolls suggested how unable to be fully alive and/or how confined by my parents' expectations I'd always been.

In the next few days I did find the voice I needed to break up with the psychoanalyst. Work on the autobiographical novel continued.

Background:

The crux of the conflict that ultimately led to my anorexia nervosa, and later to writer's block, was the way I'd learned about my father's first marriage and the way that shocking news had been kept secret and never dealt with in our family. When I was four and my mother was pregnant with my youngest sister, my eight-years-older hero and half-sister Bibba came to the yard one afternoon and shocked me with the startling news that she was not my sister, that Mommy was not her mother, and that her real mother, Babs, had died because a baby Father had put inside her with his penis had broken her open. There seemed no way out but to confront Father about what I considered to be his crime—killing women by peeing inside them. So I did so that very night. When he was alone having his drink before supper, I braced myself and asked, "Did you love Babs?" and was surprised when in the midst of tears, Father replied softly, "I loved her very much." I knew to speak of this to no one; my younger sisters only learned about the circumstances of Babs' death from me as adults. But the consequences of this secret began to take their toll on my life the very next morning when my mother, as usual, dialed up her mother in New Jersey and handed me the receiver. I was then, for the first time after having enjoyed this earlier, too afraid to talk on the phone to my Granny. Mommy had to talk for me. Only many years later did I discover in psychoanalysis that the likely unconscious reasons for that fear were: (a) terror of the power of my own voice because of the huge effect it had had on Father the night before and the belief that it had destroyed our family as I knew it, and (b) fear of Mommy witnessing the power that had made Father show his love for another woman and made me love him and want to be like that other woman.

Also related to this fear and centrally related to my subsequent fear of FAT is the conflict which developed between my belief that I was worthless and my determination to improve myself. This ultimately resulted in successes and recognition that made me feel I was receiving much more than I deserved—an heinous crime in our family and a major component in both my anorexia and my writing inhibition.

Example #7

November 24, 1991

In early November 1991, I mailed the revised and shorter autobiographical novel to my former literary agent. This felt especially important because I had been voted Distinguished Friend of Psychoanalysis by the American Psychoanalytic Association and did not want that honor for serving others to interfere with taking care of myself. Anticipating meeting with my literary agent while in New York to receive the award, I dreamed:

> I went to see Murphy Evans (a former neighbor). Directly in front of me sitting like a Buddha, he seemed fine. But looking closer, I could see his wrists were bandaged…Then, in my office (only it was in our house on Garfield Street in Washington), I was going out at 6:00 p.m. to play with the analysts. But I stashed my wallet in the back of the bottom desk drawer along with my pretty blue denim dancing bootlets. Clear, maybe bullet-proof plastic covered this drawer. Outside I could see the analysts I normally didn't know, because this was the only time they came out of their offices.

Dream Aftermath

Murphy Evans, who had selflessly devoted his life to a family business, had recently actually been attacked by a thief. I thought the dream depicted confronting the good son in me whose writing had been injured but was no longer in a cast. Pleased to note that the walking/writing boots had been replaced by durable but pretty dancing shoes inspired by the dream of one year earlier, I wondered why my valuables (writing, sexuality, self-esteem?) had to be hidden in the bottom drawer under bullet-proof plastic. For preservation's sake? To save myself from attack by Father if they were discovered? To protect myself from guilt? Or something else not yet considered?

Background:

The fact that the second half of this dream was set in Washington, D.C. is illustrative of Morton Reiser's description of how experiences are stored in our brains according to the emotions that accompanied them. During World War II, our family lived in Washington, because Father was Executive Assistant and later Press Secretary for President Roosevelt. In that period when we had no servants and no automobile, I, aged seven to eleven, experienced more independence than during any other time in my childhood. Freed from the confines of our walled garden (where I often had to stay alone before first grade) and from the social rigidity of Raleigh, I walked many places alone, had an array of friends, and enjoyed more autonomy and confidence than ever before. I was also very successful in school and in writing. My grandfather even printed a poem I'd written about the war on the editorial page of our newspaper back in Raleigh.

The contrast of hands injured but no longer confined inside a cast is illustrative of (a) hands being a symbol for my writing, and (b) how the transformation of such symbols in dreams demonstrates changed feelings in relation to them.

Example #8

December 29, 1991

That December two different agents judged my autobiographical novel not publishable in its present form. Both said it included two stories that interfered with each other, and suggested that a memoir would work better if I felt I could tolerate the public exposure. Returning home feeling devastated, I dreamed:

> An old lady was kept in solitary confinement by this sinister old man who may have been a doctor. I visited her. She was not only old but in poor health; she may have been crotchety. When I left, I realized that her keeper was going to kill her. Perhaps out of rage or exasperation or to get her money or to just get rid of her. I was horrified, but didn't know whether to tell anyone or not. If I did, the hateful keeper might deny it or charge me with libel or get me charged as an accomplice. I was also afraid that if I didn't and they found out I'd known, they'd charge me with murder, too. And not telling would make me feel *terribly, terribly* guilty.

Dream Aftermath

I had no trouble seeing the confined woman as myself. On the couch, I realized that Dr. H. was right: he, by working with me, *was* killing that isolated person. But my most sensational insight was recognizing the dream's intense terror and guilt as the same feelings that had tormented me during anorexia. Deciding that they must also be the confiners of my writing, I wondered about the relation of fear and guilt to the bottom drawer (degraded writing and self-esteem?) and bullet-proof cover (see-throughable but untouchable?) of my earlier dream. The next challenge seemed to be to get out. But how? The agents' advice had left me in intense conflict about whether to convert the novel into a memoir or give up on it and start something new.

Example #9

July 12, 1992

Further insight into what might be keeping me confined came from a dream about a clinic where I went to receive "heart medicine," but was prevented from having an appointment by a brute of a doctor. I decided that this heart medicine was something like Drano; I needed it to clean out the love for Father that still clogged my writing "equipment." During this period I began doing more public speaking; on one occasion I spoke as a writer for the first time in decades. By chance, this speaking engagement was accompanied by such severe pain in my left thumb that I subsequently consulted a hand specialist who X-rayed it, gave me a splint and a steroid injection, and told me this problem could be corrected with surgery if it continued to bother me. Associating this pain (in the thumb I had once sucked to silence myself as a child) with my speech as a woman writer connected it, also, with my earlier dream about having my right wrist in a cast. Despite the doctor's X-ray and physiological explanation for my problem, I was able to use this pain (which came and went over the next few years) to think about the possible painful loss of that thumb to my unconscious. If I should become free to speak and write as I chose, this "stopper" would no longer be needed.

That summer I hired an editor to read for me. Then, after completing and rewriting a short story, I resolved to convert the novel to memoir. In a few weeks this dream followed:

> I gave up an important suitcase or pocketbook—like my neat, versatile, roll-aboard suitcase-luggage carrier. Then I was kneeling down naked and all folded up on myself on the floor of Dr. H.'s office. Wet all over and weeping mightily about this loss, with my back to Dr. H., my scrunched-up-ness felt like I had been inside the suitcase myself…Next, I was with my artist friend, Eleanor, outdoors beside a pair of trees a few feet apart. A board was nailed to and joined these trees. Looking at the board, Eleanor saw this scary children's art work (clay monster faces) on it that she loved. A little boy who lived with elves under the roots of one tree had made this art. Eleanor wanted to leave a note to him on the back of one of her pictures to say how much she liked his work. I knew this boy and suggested to Eleanor that she tell him in her note that she was a friend of mine. But she didn't want to…Then I went out in the garage of our Shamrock Drive house, in a nightgown you could not see through, to meet a friend. But before she arrived, a cute little four-year-old blond girl came up with this long-haired, pimply-faced, flaky-looking pedophile. He introduced both of them to me, "I'm a bigamist who lives up the

hill there by Adelaide, and she's the daughter of my neighbor, the kidnap-per."...Then riding to the airport at night in a van with lots of other people, I feared I had forgotten my bags. We stopped and turned on the lights to look. I *had* left the roller one, but I still had the red canvas carry-on with two han-dles. As we drove away, there were long lines of traffic at the pay booths, but the middle lane was clear for us.

Dream Aftermath

Out of the *suit*case used to ward off attacks by trying to please both parents at once, it was obvious that I was going to feel like a vulnerable, skinned, and deformed creature, unequipped to function in the world. The board nailed to the two trees was at the same height as when the hammock in the yard of my child-hood had been pushed hard enough to enable us to exhilaratingly bring back "money" in the form of leaves. I soon recognized the board as "bored," which I had used much of my life to ward off the terrifying emotional attacks by my par-ents that had inevitably followed moments of success and exhilaration. I won-dered, but did not understand why, the artist-in-me would not let the present me be in touch with the boy artist under the roots. The bigamist would be my father, in my child's mind married to my mother and his first wife all at once and, there-fore, available to me in identifying with the latter. The nightgown that could not be seen through suggested, however, that other things continued to be kept out of my awareness. Still, the ease of getting through toll booths made me think I might have become able to take more in stride whatever losses had to be "paid."

Background:

This long dream contained a whole series of images that I would refer back to again and again. Here, too, was where I began to appreciate the creativeness of dream images and language. Seeing the "board" with scary art at the height I associated with exhilaration made me understand, as never before, how afraid I was of excitement and success. "Suitcase" was an even more vivid label for the cast in the April 1989 dream.

Example #10–#12

September 9–September 21, 1992

As I contemplated converting autobiographical novel to memoir, a series of dreams following the one about getting out of the suitcase enlightened me about the mix of emotions involved. First there was one about bringing a tiny white elephant girl to life. In that dream people were saying she would need lots of guidance because she didn't have judgment about heights and taking care of herself, a premonition that proved to be extremely helpful in waking life. As I toyed with ways to convert, I found removing the novel's outer shell a surprisingly easy task. But interweaving past and present in the memoir so that each informed the other brought both a new experience of writing effectively and intense aching of a depressive and almost physical flulike nature. This pain would cease at the completion of each rewrite session, but loom up to possess me again when I resumed the process. But the sense of myself or the writing as weak or dead had vanished. As I actually began this conversion, I dreamed:

9/9/92

It was on the news that the earth had grown larger. This meant to me that it could barrel out to the edge of space and fall over the side. I was too terrified to read any more about it. But then I was relieved to hear other people talking who'd read in *Newsweek* that space was infinite and that, therefore, barreling out to new parts of it didn't mean falling over the side.

Dream Aftermath

This dream let me both recognize my terror and ease it.

9/11/92

There was this *high* cliff. Out on 70 West. Near Napier's gas station and the turnoff to where we used to live. I was up *on* it, looking down, almost like seeing the road from the top of a high wall. I was driving my present car—white Honda with sun roof—with *somebody* in the passenger's seat. Suddenly I realized I could fly down and land on the highway heading west. To do so would be exciting and much easier than driving the long way around. In one way I knew I could do it because I had before—twice in smaller jumps. But I was too scared this time to try.

Dream Aftermath

This dream helped me see that converting the novel to memoir psychologically resembled the freeing effort of commuting to the University of North Carolina at Chapel Hill to get my B.A. and then my PhD. That had been *hard,* from age 36 to 43, with four children, getting divorced in the process, and after a 20-year break from school. But I'd done it. Therefore, I believed, this conversion, though scary, might similarly be accomplished and help free me. I went on working at it, but in a *slow,* roundabout way as the dream suggested. And this triggered the next dream:

9/21/92

> I needed to get back to Carolina Country Club and my room there. It was suppertime and people were lined up getting food. I didn't know how to properly get back in. I wasn't so much concerned with how I looked (which was a bit disheveled from walking back from Butner carrying shoes, underpants, a book, and wearing only a longish T-shirt) as with not disrupting the propriety of the club.

Dream Aftermath

Although preoccupied with the creative process of converting novel to more self-revealing memoir, at the unconscious level I clearly felt this was a repeat of bringing a book I'd written back from a mental hospital to the affluently proper world of my family. Butner was the location of a state mental hospital where I had worked during my training. I had always privately detested what seemed to me the haughty pretentiousness of the Carolina Country Club, though I would have been humiliated by presenting myself nearly naked anywhere. But while this dream represented both these negative feelings, it also had two positive aspects that, by then, I was able to recognize and use appreciatively: first, I *was* walking independently back from the mental hospital, and second, I was *not* wearing "under" pants (which could keep me an "underdog"). At that time I did not think about the implications of thus exposing myself sexually. Instead, I recalled the mix of excitement and humiliation I'd felt with the publication of my first and best-selling novel which I'd written while hospitalized.

These insights about the emotions stirred up in me, I am convinced, made it easier to continue writing. Even now, reviewing these dreams and writing about the process reminds me that converting novel to memoir must have also resembled converting a mental patient to a young woman in the world.

<u>*Background:*</u>

These dreams illustrate the inner stress and distress that accompanied converting my novel to memoir. Since I'd written <u>Caleb, My Son</u> while in the psychiatric hospital, only to be surprised after discharge when it was published and became a best seller, it was not surprising that the feelings from that time would accompany my efforts to put a new "first" book out now.

Example #13

<u>August 17, 1993</u>

With continued work on the memoir, I arrived at a place where I wanted to see my treatment records from all the various places I'd seen doctors and/or been hospitalized. This required several months and sometimes persistence with the help of my lawyer. When I finally did receive the records from New York Hospital at White Plains, I was overwhelmed with shock, anger, and a new recognition of what terrible things had befallen me. I doubt that the dream that came a few days later would have been so helpfully revealing without that reaction:

> I lost all my money. It was awful! Devastating. Because losing my money was retroactive. It wasn't just becoming poor now. It was like dominoes falling backward. Without it I couldn't pay for education or analysis or have children or be a psychologist. I was *nothing*. My life was empty and *ruined*.

<u>Dream Aftermath</u>

Before this dream the writing had been going relatively well. After it, writing went splendidly despite eating out of control and my very distressed reaction to that. I did understand, however, that I felt as though writing successfully, like this realization of the terrible mistreatment I'd suffered when hospitalized, was causing me to lose my life as I knew it. *I was losing my whole basis for existing.* More specifically, writing effectively made me feel, at the unconscious level, that I was losing the dutiful helplessness that I believed had made me valuable to my parents. How could I go on after this? How could I ever put this identity behind me and go forward, free of it?

Background:

The most upsetting thing learned from reading my hospital records was that I had been diagnosed "dementia praecox" (another name for schizophrenia). Worse still, the basis for this diagnosis was a delusion I'd talked about after many ECT treatments had erased my thought processes. This delusion was that little men were in my throat and stomach. Since I had no psychotherapy in the hospital, no doctor ever understood (until my analyst thirty years later) how those little men related to the elves under the roots of the trees Bibba had talked to me about at age three and four. At that time, too, Bibba had told me she could make me as small as those elves and cause me to be invisible like them. It now seems likely that I associated the doctors' ECT and insulin shock with the magical conversion I'd feared from Bibba in early childhood.

With hindsight, the fact that I was "diagnosed" and not treated in relation to my talk of these little men is even more appalling because at age twenty, when I was resigned to being a hospital "lifer," I designed and created a five by seven foot rug related to the issue. No psychiatrist there ever asked me about it. Yet had they done so, I'm sure I would have readily and naively poured out the story behind it. And from that story any dynamic-thinking therapist could have pieced together the basis of the anorexia nervosa that had nearly killed me. Here is a photo of the rug.

Example #14

October 25, 1993

As I continued working at the memoir and prepared and presented more public talks, situations arose that made me aware of feeling competitive with my sisters but inadequate in comparison. In analysis, I also came to understand how terrified I'd always been that I might voice the secret I'd learned about Father and Babs (that he had loved Babs more than Mommy). In this context, and with writing much easier, I dreamed:

> A *terrible* dream that was mostly just feelings. No action. I was horribly injured and mutilated in my mouth, neck, chest and arms. Like I'd been bludgeoned with a club. All this had to do with my voice. I was trying to decide whether to speak out and feel the pain of struggling toward recovery or to just remain silent. Speaking out would both hurt to the quick and display my mutilation.

Dream Aftermath

I kept this dream in mind as I worked to become more proficient as a public speaker. Doing so, I realized, would amount to both becoming more like Father and giving up being Babs, the dead woman he'd loved.

I considered also that, if I recognized this memoir as an accomplishment, my parents inside me would also recognize this and react. Because the book would be, unconsciously, like a baby and, therefore, proof of sex with Father, it would turn both parents against me. I decided I needed to remember that a book is a book, *not* a baby. At this time, too, I was aware of myself deliberately emotionally confronting and moving apart from my mother (who had been dead fourteen years).

Background:

Because both my parents were so emotionally involved in my writing, freedom to write for myself would require more than the usual efforts to separate. Besides Father's warmth and pride mixed with jealous cruelty, I was tied to him through fear and sexual attraction. At the same time, Mommy's narcissistic praise and her harsh aggressiveness in urging me to achieve had made me not want to be an "alive" woman (like her!). Obviously I would need to claim, feel, and not be controlled by these emotions if I were ever to feel comfortable as a writer or a woman.

Example #15

January 5, 1994

Still converting novel to memoir, I discovered many complex feelings about my voice and my strength belonging to *me* and in opposition to my parents. Considering anorexia as, among other things, my form of defiance, I concluded in the copybook: "Fear and inadequacy have been my conscious representations of unconscious defiance. Anorexia condensed the two; it was the strongest, most compelling and most devastating 'cryptosymbol.' It converted 'not being able to speak' downward to 'not begin able to eat.'"

At this point, I realized that I could now write and write, but *showing* myself in writing or in any other way remained both scary and disruptive. A dream illustrated this:

> In the middle of the night. Me as a child being forced to say the "right" thing in a way I wasn't capable and that would kill me. I was strangling on those words while my parents stood over me, demanding that I say them perfectly even though they could see I was going to die from trying.

Dream Aftermath

I continued to work on these same issues. As I wrote more easily, wishes to eat and drink more than I felt was right plagued me. At the point of sending the memoir to my agent, I realized that I was in the process of losing or giving up the fantasy of NOT BEING A WRITER.

Example #16

July 25, 1995

Much had transpired in a little over a year. I had sent the memoir to my agent who wanted to represent it. I'd also worked with an editor he'd recommended. Now the agent was peddling a sleeker, slightly shorter version to publishers. And I, finally free of this project, had begun work on a collection of short stories. In addition, I had to spend some of my free (non-clinical) time writing speeches. Being hopeful about the short stories and more comfortable as a speaker made all of this easier. About seven weeks before this next dream, I'd had surgery to correct the crippling cartilage failure in my left thumb that had been diagnosed two years earlier.

> At a hotel. There was going to be a big party with important people somewhere else. This party had to do with me, but I wasn't going. In this dream I saw my mother looking primly sophisticated and very frail. She said she had two things wrong with her—as if they were both minor. I can't recall one, but the other was "pancreatic." (That disturbed me both in the dream and on awakening. I thought of pancreatic cancer.)
>
> At one point, while still preparing for the party I wasn't going to, I got my secretary's convertible out of storage. It looked kind of drab and seedy parked outside under two trees. There were two lumps sitting on its hood. Looked at more closely, one turned out to be a horse chestnut. The other was a weird little animal with arms and legs like a person, but all loose-jointed so that they wouldn't support him. His whole body shape was concealed by long (as long as his body), all-consuming, greasy brown hair. I was afraid to touch either lump. They looked, at first glance, like globs of Spanish moss.

Dream Aftermath

Awake, I thought about "pancreatic" and realized that in dream language it could also mean "all creative." And, of course, if I were to be "all creative," my mother's rigid control would die. Interesting to prepare for a party I wasn't going to; I'd always felt that way about my successes and my mother. Her lavish and narcissistically exulting praise had so humiliated me as a small child that I'd invented the fantasy of turning to water and leaking away through the floorboards. I knew that a convertible must signal some change in myself. Curious about the horse chestnut and the weird animal on the car's hood, I soon made a heartwarming discovery: another name for horse chestnut is "buck eye," which was still very much a problem I needed to overcome, *refusing to receive recognition*. And that weird little creature would be me as "greasy grind." Clearly this dream was showing me that to convert myself into the writer I wanted to be, I would need to confront and deal with all of these negative associations and responses to my own success. Specifically I would need to grapple with and leave behind "buck eye" and "greasy grind."

Example #17

March 30, 1996

With continued work at both writing and speaking, some success was inevitable. The memoir had not yet sold, but when a short story in progress went well and we had a very successful annual conference (where I also spoke) at the Lucy Daniels Foundation, I dreamed:

> I was diddling my feet extended up into the air trying to get them unentangled from some yarn or string (feet straight up like one of the back exercises I do). By accident (I didn't notice he was there) my foot bumped into the face of a man who was sitting at the Shamrock Drive dining room table.
>
> I was in the Shamrock Drive living room just the other side of the French doors between it and the dining room. Down on the floor. I heard a huge crash from outside the dining room. Great impact and shattering glass caused by something barreling in from the terrace. I was *terrified!* *What* was it? A car or huge animal breaking into the dining room. *By accident or on purpose?* Still crawling on the floor, I opened the French doors from the living room slightly to see. A man with a funny head—maybe just a spool or a giant odd-shaped helmet that covered his whole face and head—was charging at me with a big bludgeoning weapon. I could hardly (being paralyzed by fear) get myself together to defend myself. He towered above me as I was still down on the floor. He approached to slaughter me. I screamed for help while desperately trying to fight him off. In the end I had a large thing like a knife that was really just a spatula…

I woke briefly.

> Back asleep: It was my birthday. At a busy place noisy with a lot of people, I was going off in a car with my mother and somebody else to get ready for the afternoon. I planned to take a short nap, then a shower, then get my degree, and then perform in some way. Mommy said this was too much to do in a day. She suggested that I get my degree another day. This made me mad. I saw putting off getting my degree as potentially destructive procrastination. I told her, "No. I'm going to both get my degree and do the performance afterward." I was also supposed to leave on a train that night.

Dream Aftermath

Note the contrast of this dream with the ones I'd had earlier in my writing process. In addition to being able to symbolize the fight with my father in this dream, other confrontations—like kicking the man in the face, crawling, hearing a crash in the dining room, opposing my mother—were imaged in a way that allowed me greater possibility of recognizing and dealing with fear and aggression.

But I also gained other valuable insights with this dream. Two days later I was stricken with painful and incapacitating back spasms. I had suffered these several times before and had learned to do daily exercises to prevent them. Straining agonizingly to get up off the floor from doing these exercises, I realized that I was in the same position as I'd been in in the dream! This led me to consider, as I never had before, that some of the stress that caused these back spasms might come from the very successes I was working to have. Of course, this realization made it seem all the more necessary to keep going.

The dream's setting—the Shamrock Drive house, where I'd ended an abusive marriage and turned my life around with the hard-earned freedom of going back to college and acquiring my doctorate in clinical psychology—also provided a hopeful reminder.

Background:

Another interesting thing about the back spasms is that my father had suffered from them as well. In fact, one of the traumatic moments of my childhood had been hearing him cry out in agony from the shower when I was nine. I thought he was dying. Since my mother was out, I had to go in and help him get out of the shower and dry off. The whole time I felt trapped between my duty to keep him from dying and my guilt over being with him naked. A few months later, when I was deathly ill with the measles, I feared I would die or go blind because of having seen him naked.

Example #18

<u>October 19, 1996</u>

I continued work on the short story collection, completing one story after another interspersed with going back to rework stories previously completed. I felt relatively good about this effort and its products, even though I'd begun to realize that publishers were not going to buy my memoir. Working on a story called "Golden Wedding," I felt desperately out of control and then dreamed:

> I got out of my car at the corner of Harvey and Caswell Sts. with the car fully headed into Caswell. I was standing beside it, but the car rolled forward away from me and had a small accident (with its driver's side door open) in front of my parents' house. Probably it hit one parked car, but I can't remember.
>
> Weeks later (so long that I'd forgotten the other time), I got out of my car at the same spot while it was running. I knew I shouldn't, maybe it was even in gear and I jumped out expecting to jump right in again and it got away from me. I saw it rolling pretty fast and chose not to run to try to catch it (which would have been impossible) and just prayed it wouldn't crash. But other cars were coming out at the time, and I watched a three or four car pile-up with mine. I felt awful from this point on in the dream. People came out and spoke to me about it. I was apologizing and relieved no one was hurt or killed. But the other people were much more serious; they had planned to confront me before this last wreck and now really planned to, much as you might confront someone about damaging behavior when drunk.
>
> These neighbors were also having a party and invited me to come. There I continued to feel terrible as they pleasantly and kindly alluded to how this second crash made the earlier less damaging one more serious. I needed to do something about myself. They seemed kind, however; they offered me party food in a neighborly way. One young man (who I guess was a doctor) demonstrated to me that one patient couldn't have a particular type of inner experience because drugs, disease, or genetics had erased the brain area needed for it. For a while I was holding this darling little boy baby that looked like a doll. He had a flat head with almost no hair on it, but a fringe of hair growing around the sides. He had on red plaid overalls and a white shirt. He had a necklace of gold beads (like the one I gave my daughter Lucy) around his neck. He also had a whole set of gold teeth inside his mouth. When I saw these, I pointed them out to people. He smiled a lot and was dear to hold and play with. Just before leaving I gave him to someone else to hold.
>
> This was a very wealthy, comfortable family with integrity. They could be decent to me while also having been hurt by and disapproving of my behavior. They didn't openly confront me at their party but did let me know with dis-

crete soberness that they would need to later. At the same time, the mother let me know about some luxurious services she used that I might be interested in. Near time to leave they wanted me to have some food. I didn't want to (to not feel fat and because I didn't like it). They had liver and some dark bread sandwiches.

Dream Aftermath

These wrecks, like successful writing, had caused me much shame (related to Mommy) and guilt (related to Father) but had not done serious damage. I interpreted my getting out of the moving car as getting out of the identity my parents expected me to have—maybe by publishing both my novels or both these new books. Maybe this was another form of breaking out of the suitcase. Nevertheless, the baby with the gold necklace and gold teeth made me think of myself as still enamored of being my parents' "favorite son."

Example #19

February 9, 1997

I mailed off the manuscript of the short story collection. In doing so, I felt like a monstrous animal who ate too much, wrote too much, and farted too much. Yes, a bottomless pit, I could swallow houses and whole towns without touching my hunger. In this context I dreamed:

> I drove up to an intersection in the Research Triangle after a *very* hectic day at the LDF. I was going pretty fast, but stopped appropriately, though with a jolt, assisted by a parking bar (as in my garage). I thought about how I had stopped and not had an accident and was relieved to not feel guilty...
>
> Then I arrived home, a combination of my present house and the Shamrock Drive one where I raised the children. It had been thoroughly cleaned up and cleaned out. In the living room I turned on the TV and then muted it. Upstairs my (Shamrock Drive) bedroom also looked cleaned up and cleaned out. Looking over from my bed toward the window seat, I saw this china statue of a dachshund on the rug where Persephone, my children's beloved pet, should be. Seeing this ceramic dachshund made me feel intense sadness, loss, guilt, and anger. I realized that Persephone was lost and that whoever had cleaned up the house was trying to act like that didn't matter. I felt *terrible* for not preventing this loss, and I hated whoever had cleaned out the house and was trying to make me accept this lifeless sham in Persephone's place.

Dream Aftermath

It occurred to me that the dachshund lost was more like Persephone, our children's pet, than Hansel, the dog that had been my childhood companion in the yard. Thus, she represented female me. Perhaps, with my fourth book now off to the agent and a fifth one planned, I felt like the Persephone (silenced) me was lost. Also, writing like this would make me like the reverse of Babs, like the beloved dead me had been lost. Yet, the ceramic figure seemed evidence of my still wishing to deny that loss.

Background:

Dachshunds have been important companions in my life since early childhood. When, as a three to six-year-old, I was locked out of our house all afternoon in our walled garden, my only company was a brown dachshund named Hansel. He was both a comfort and a playmate, even submitting at times to being dressed in doll clothes. Long after Hansel's death (the Christmas before I was hospitalized), I asked for and received a miniature dachshund named Fritz. He died in less than a year after my departure. Then our children had a brown female dachshund named Persephone. She ran the household, barking loudly if the boys played war with cap guns inside the house and bringing her food dish to you when she wanted to eat. Many years later, in the aloneness following my second divorce, I decided to try having a dog again. This time she was a miniature dachshund I named Moonshine because of her glistening black coat. The name "Moonshine" also fit her playful, fierce, affectionate spirit. She quickly became my best friend. All of these beloved short-legged creatures have contributed to my unconscious viewing of the "underdog" as lovable and, thus, to my straining to copy them to both prevent Father's jealous attacks and ward off identifying with Mommy's narcissistic haughtiness.

Example #20

<u>October 9, 1997</u>

Much was going on in my life at this time. Earlier that year I had built and moved into a new office building within a mile of my home. (My previous office of 15 years had been sold and demolished to make way for luxury condos.) My beautiful building, flooded with sunlight, was wonderful, but made me feel small, empty, undeserving, and alone, even though several colleagues I knew and liked were there with me.

That fall I had also learned from my agent that he could not sell my story collection to a commercial press but would try an academic press, if I wished. My response to this was to review the stories and decide that I didn't want them published at all because they no longer seemed good enough. (I only realized years later that academic publishers were nothing to be ashamed of in today's difficult publishing climate.) Further thoughts about this "failure" led me to conclude that the mix of true and fictional stories I'd been excited to create in this collection was still a "deadening" way of using "too thoughtful" me to insulate "creative me" from the world. In analysis I talked about needing to keep analytic and self-awareness efforts out of my fiction.

These thoughts and the new clinical office with a writing room off my consulting room reminded me that, though I now had my own writing room, Father was still in it. I needed to put Father (Dr. H.?) out in order to gain confidence in writing freely and not remain his "boy."

> I inherited valuable things that were brought to me by a man in an armored truck. He was to deliver and install these things for me. I may have been married in this dream. The reason I say it this way is that my husband (if I *was* married) wasn't dominant or abusive or the star; I just wasn't utterly alone…But the man who had brought this inheritance had brought more than I really deserved (or than really was mine). He had brought one piece that was sort of stolen (like off an assembly line or something there were lots of, but with one not being mine). He had also bought other things but had *not* paid the tax that was due (on their being transferred to me). When I realized this on his arrival, I felt like just going along with it. After all, *he* was the deliverer; the stealing, dishonesty and law breaking weren't my fault. But as we were going on in the few hours between when he arrived and when the inheritance would be installed, I felt terribly guilty. I knew that I was knowingly going along with his having stolen things and broken the tax law (by not paying the tax) for my benefit. If I got caught, in addition to legal penalties, there would be terrible, terrible ruckus about me in the press. If I didn't go along

and accept the extras he was bringing, I would still get my "lawful" inheritance, just much less because the taxes had been deducted. But I *wanted* it all. So I was trying to decide what to do.

Dream Aftermath

Considering this dream, I realized how guilty I must feel about all the things I was currently receiving, especially the new office and a greater capacity to write fiction. Despite the "failure" of my story collection, I had begun work on a novel that I called "Color Blind." I decided that the driver of the armored truck in the dream was Dr. H. and that the truck (analysis?) was breaking Father's law by bringing me a tax-free inheritance and an un-inherited bonus. I understood that Father's law forbade me to be my full self—woman *and* writer. Thinking more about this, I realized that my personal stories were being used to "insulate" the reader from the power of my fiction in order to prevent Father's jealous attacks as in childhood. I vowed not to repeat this insulation effort in the novel I was beginning.

Example #21

October 30, 1997

After my painful decisions about the short story collection, I felt determined to work at fiction in a way that would exclude personal analytic thought. With this in mind, I turned to the novel, my first "real" one since *High on a Hill*. Working on it, I carefully stayed with just the story and one main character, Lily. Then:

> People riding by to see a major job (accomplishment) made by me.
>
> I took my family and all our stuff and stopped (in the process of a trip) overnight at some other people's very nice house. Without their being told, without asking their permission, without my knowing them. In one way it was secret; in another it was quite out in the open. We went in the front door and made ourselves at home in part of the house without ever speaking to them. They were there in another part of the house without ever speaking to us. They had a maid as well. I felt so ashamed and embarrassed the whole time but stayed nevertheless. I also didn't really know why I was doing this.
>
> In this dream I became aware of two other small things (like brushing my teeth or tying my shoes) which I wasn't being responsible with either. I stayed there but kept sneaking around, afraid of getting caught or, especially, of coming face to face with the woman (wife) of the house. I also thought about trying to make myself feel better later by tipping her maid and/or sending her a thank-you present. I was most afraid of bumping into her in the house because I didn't know how in the world I would explain what I was doing there. Near the end of the dream I saw her (white-haired but not old) driving away, and that was a great relief to me. I was about to leave, too. I think she might have avoided meeting me as well, because she knew I was a lady and it would be awkward. Even though she ought to be angry and confront me, that would be awkward because she knew I was a respectable person who would feel shamed by being caught in this act. So she'd feel embarrassed to confront me the way she ought to. I had small children with me as well and, at one point, I got young adults in my party to take care of them while I packed up my stuff.

Dream Aftermath

The house was probably the novel. Or the "me" writing this new novel. Considering this, I could see that both the sneaking-around me and the rightful-owner me were unable or unwilling to claim themselves. In fact, the rightful-owner me needed to put the sneaking-around me out of her house. Her not doing so reminded me of how my father had hidden his and my mother's glasses of Bourbon behind the books in our library whenever my teetotaler grandfather unexpectedly dropped by for a visit. That had shocked and amazed me in childhood; it was so at odds with Father's usual brash confrontiveness. As an adult, I knew that I would have felt humiliated doing such a thing. Yes, in my writing as well as in my life, *I* needed to claim and take full responsibility for my power, my anger, my sexuality. In not doing so, I'd kept myself and my writing weak and humiliated, hiding my writing like Father had hidden his Bourbon.

Background:

Grandfather Josephus Daniels was a newspaper editor and statesman who remained true to his Methodist principles wherever he was. Besides being a teetotaler, as Secretary of the Navy under Woodrow Wilson, he took wine rations away from the enlisted men. However, his tendency was to act, not to preach. Had my parents drunk their Bourbon in his presence, I believe he would have said nothing. In his later years he was known to encourage house guests to go visit his sons around the cocktail hour. "I know they'll be looking for you a little after five," he'd say.

Example #22

December 19, 1997

Besides work on the novel, I was also giving more talks for the Lucy Daniels Foundation. With more practice, this speaking grew easier even though the occasions I spoke at were more challenging. One of these was a presentation during the meetings of the American Psychoanalytic Association in New York. Prior to that and speaking to the LDF advisory board in a SoHo Art gallery, I dreamed:

> At the Lucy Daniels Foundation, I saw at a distance this huge black close-cropped kinky-haired creature. He looked like a camel with its hump misplaced backward. But he was black and much bigger than a camel. He also looked like a giant dog, a monstrosity—huge, black, like both a camel and a Labrador retriever, as well as not really either. A frightening but compelling freak. Outside with him, I did my best to stay at a distance and out of his sight. He was not looking for me, but I had the feeling that he might be hungry and attack or swallow you on the spur of the moment, without pre-meditation. He also had a dirty, white-greying, worn bandage tied around his front right ankle. This seemed to show that, at least for a few minutes, he had let people close enough to help him. However, he was a unique creature never seen before by anyone; his habits, characteristics, and way of behaving were completely unknown. And I was both afraid and very attracted to this oddity. Outside, I struggled to keep the camel from seeing me or coming to or bumping into me.
>
> Inside the LDF, where I went to get safety from the camel, I was still afraid in this mostly glass building. I feared the camel's breaking through the glass, being rabid, trampling me down, eating me up, etc. At one point the camel came inside, too, but with a little guidance from me and others went uneventfully out again. When it was outside again and I was inside, I did all manner of things (like lie down on the floor) to keep it from seeing and coming at me through the glass. Again, the feelings were strong and complex: I feared and was drawn to (in an almost loving way) this monstrosity; I was afraid to even be seen by it because there was *literally* no telling what it might do if it realized it wasn't alone in the world.

Dream Aftermath

I thought the black camel was a representation not only of me as a black sheep but also, of my creativity, my imagination. Clearly I feared them all. I also thought the bandage on the camel's paw was significant in its similarity to my November 24, 1991 dream and my April 1989 hand in a cast dream. The fact that it was dirty and that the camel was using that foot as well as the other three suggested that the bandage was no longer needed, but that he just couldn't get close enough to someone like myself for them to take it off. I decided then that this dream's important message was: "I am so afraid of recognizing and being in touch with my creativity (voice and images) that I don't let myself close enough to remove the no-longer-needed cast-bandage-crippler." This also reminded me of the March 30, 1996 dream. Comparing the two, I realized that whereas the issue in the 1996 dream had been separation and "getting my degree," the issue now seemed to be finding a way to get close enough to touch, speak with, and no longer fear this creature that reminded me of the black dog flying over cacti on a quilt I had hanging in my library.

When I talked to Dr. H. about this dream, he wondered whether the camel was a representation of my aloneness. From that perspective, the bandage on its paw could be evidence of at least one attempt to relate to another (perhaps Dr. H. himself). I knew, listening, that Dr. H. was right and that his objective perspective enabled him to put into words the aspects of the dream I found most profound and difficult to bear.

Example #23

March 19, 1998

Other events interacting with the novel work made me feel "too indulgent," "too fat." Meanwhile in analysis, I had become clear that I could not accept myself as a writer or be a writer because to do so would make me unacceptable to the "Father" inside me. I understood, too, that feeling "FAT" was a response to my own effort to break out of his control. Considering this, I recalled Father's ridiculing me into eating shad roe at age 3 or 4. Afraid to take fish eggs inside me because of having recently learned about babies growing from an egg inside the mother, I had, nevertheless, numbed out my tongue and throat and swallowed the shad roe to stop Father's angry taunting. Now I could articulate that discovery made in childhood: words in my mouth could set Father off, whereas food in my stomach shut him up.

> I was out in the world (a New York City or Raleigh street) creating—making things or paintings. I went to a room in a building off one side street. Along with me, perhaps with me showing or setting the example for them, was this other person. The whole thing was dangerous. Maybe I was looking for refuge. We went to another place where another creative person was busy creating (maybe at my place at my parents' dining room table). I was somewhere else, maybe the kitchen. Suddenly, I got caught in this trap set by the person out to get us. Ropes, hanging from a door frame, suddenly wrapped around my neck. In the doorway between the kitchen and the dining room, I was being strangled and screaming for help. Only after a long time did the other person (who was at the table creating) come and save me.

Dream Aftermath

This dream portrayed two parts of me, the writing me and the scared me looking for refuge. Though it would make sense to seek refuge at home, given my particular experience there, it also made sense that home was where I expected attack. But interestingly, the creative part of me at the table was not the me who got attacked. It was the walking me who was leaving the kitchen. Being strangled made sense, given my voice conflict. I was being hung but this hanging failed. The gallows didn't work.

So, basically, it was just *fear* that plagued me. In analysis, I realized that my life is more terrifying because I can't count on myself to take care of me and this terror probably interferes with many things I want to do. This led me to think for days about the issue of oral aggression: my father's angry ridicule of me and my own silence; also, my compulsive eating and blocked writing as both damage he'd done to me and my own aggressive response. As I continued work on speeches and the novel, it finally occurred to me that what I needed to do was USE my oral greed and rage (aggression) to become a more effective writer and speaker. I could also use this dream's imagery to help with that.

Example #24

August 17, 1998

Work on the novel continued along with speech writing and seminar preparation. With summer vacation, much more dedicated work on the novel was possible. In the context of this heavy-duty writing, I dreamed:

> I parked my car near a supermarket and needed to make purchases before I went back to it. I was going to buy or maybe I possessed two or three small golden figures like Monopoly Game playing pieces. I wanted to be sure the people knew these were legitimately mine. Then I suddenly saw on the ground a whole slew of these in a bunch, maybe a cupful. I picked them up but didn't want to be considered stealing.
>
> …There was something about going back to a summer writers' camp provided by George School. It was one month long in Maine. The neat thing about it was that, after all these years, I could go to this camp and write and talk about my feelings about having been in the hospital. Doing so would correct what happened to me at George School.

Dream Aftermath

The content of this dream impressed me as a brilliant revelation that brought past experience into the present. Being parked near the supermarket suggested being close to allowing myself power and gratification in relation to writing. So did the Monopoly pieces; their tiny size seemed related to both my lifelong need to stay small and my wish to be empowered. The concern about people thinking I was stealing might reflect ambivalence about claiming my writing. The fact that this camp (like the one I'd been sent away to for two months as a nine-year-old) could correct what had happened to me at George School suggested that this summer's writing would end the anorexia (or, in this case, writing abstinence) that had caused me to leave school and be hospitalized.

Background:

I'd been a junior at George School in fall 1949 when my first short story was published in Seventeen Magazine. I only understood in psychoanalysis forty-odd years later that the thrill and praise accompanying that event had exacerbated my anorexia (first diagnosed in 1946 but never treated). My condition had so deteriorated by spring 1950 that the school insisted I have treatment before I returned for my senior year. I never did return because life at home was more than I could bear. By the fol-

lowing spring (1951, when I should have graduated) I had lost another 40 pounds (I was down to just over 50 pounds), and was hospitalized.

Example #25

September 18, 1998

As I continued regular, dedicated work on the novel, it seemed to develop in a way that made me feel adequate and productive, and that gave me a sense that what was being turned out was good enough. In the midst of this, I began to ache physically and emotionally with depression and sadness, though I did not stop writing. Then I dreamed:

> My hands were so sore that I consulted a doctor about them. He said, "There's nothing wrong with your hands." "But they're red," I implored, holding them out.

Dream Aftermath

Again, like a light flashing on! This dream made it even clearer than the feelings themselves that writing productively made me ache with sadness. In my effort to understand, I realized that productive writing would eventually make me lose myself as the crippled-writer I'd believed Father could love.

Example #26

November 16, 1998

Productive writing continued. I sometimes even felt like a writer.

> Driving (away from the office, perhaps), I found myself in the midst of a horrible wreck, a pile-up with cars wrecked and people badly injured both in front of me and behind. I managed to extricate both myself and my car and drive away. But I felt terribly, terribly, terribly guilty; also like I was going to get caught, that the police would discover I'd been in the accident and blame me for the whole thing. I didn't know *what* to do, but thought about going back to tell them before they came for me. Then—and I am not clear whether this was inside the dream or outside it—I realized (maybe because I went back and saw inside myself) that it was just a dream and that if I went back I would not only get in trouble (unnecessarily) but embarrass myself.

Dream Aftermath

The wreck and the guilt finally revealed the damage and the self-blame I unconsciously dread with writing effectively. At the same time, despite its being an afterthought, I felt empowered by not having to go back and claim responsibility for things that weren't really my fault.

Example #27

January 13, 1999

The novel continued to grow in size and scope. It was not perfect; in fact, it had turned into a much more mammoth undertaking than I'd envisioned. Nevertheless the work was engrossing. At times I felt comfortable and competent as a writer despite knowing I was far from finished.

> A tall, delicate blond man came to my bed at night and lay down very close to me. It was like he was coming back after a fight or after fear or some other problem…After a few minutes of quiet physical closeness, the light came on and together we looked at the barely visible thread-like shape that appeared to be created by the light. Only outside the dream later was I able to make that shape out as a megaphone or maybe a telescope. Then we looked at a set of images, each put into words on tiny separate sheets of paper…Later this delicate man, who reminded me of St. Exupery's Little Prince grown up, stood with his arms around me, still in my bedroom. Clearly we loved each other. But suddenly, to my surprise, he told me he was going away for a while. This hurt me, and I asked how long. "Just four days," he said. "Till the weekend." When I told him I didn't like him to be away, he said, "But I have to. I'm a nervous wreck here with you. Because I'm afraid." His response did not make me feel that I was to blame. I could understand that he wanted to be close to me, but had to leave because fear of loving me made him behave a way he couldn't tolerate.

Dream Aftermath

Another surprise. I understood from this dream that despite loving the writing, I was afraid to love it or to feel loved by it. Representing the writing as a tender lover also allowed me to consider the sweetness it held for me as well as my fear of being seduced by it.

Example #28

January 18, 1999

Productive writing continued. A few days later I dreamed:

> My father, who had grown old and haggard and had strangely shrunk to be a disheveled dwarf, was traveling with a woman. He stopped on the way and came up to me wearing a wide-brimmed hat and holding out a precious gift. It was a crude triangular-shaped clay-colored stone dangling from a hook. A poem was engraved in it in script. But when I read the poem, it was oddly disappointing. It neither rhymed nor made a meaningful point.

Dream Aftermath

In the midst of writing effectively, I still longed for Father's "gift"—dead, meaningless writing that would keep me an Oedipal stone, a treasure for Father, and help me not lose the deadly "love" he could bestow on me. But at least this dream allowed me to see my self-destructive wishes and not just remain blindly controlled by them.

Example #29

March 31, 1999

By this time I had completed two very different drafts of the novel and was looking closely at organizational and possible point of view changes. These were challenging and thought-provoking, sometimes exciting, but not discouraging.

> I was sleeping alone (in the little sewing room I slept in as a small child after I was moved out of the nursery) because Tom didn't come to bed. I had a distressing dream. In the dream I had a big belt (like Father's) around me like a hoolahoop. Maybe I was doing a twisting-turning dance (like Bibba did when I was a little girl and she sang that song about "In the southern part of France where the ladies wear no pants, they do the hootchie-kootchie when they dance"). This was somehow very distressing. When I woke up and found myself alone (with some little white package or gift deposited at the crack of the nearly closed door), I kept wanting to tell this to people who didn't really want to listen. Tom was one of them.

Dream Aftermath

This dream excited me, because I knew it would reveal liberating information. That was the room I'd slept in at age four when my youngest sister, Cleves, was born. The night of her birth I was alone in the house with Father. This scared me, probably because I'd learned that his first wife had died when a baby he'd put inside her had broken her open as it came out. Perhaps, too, because of Father's raucous ways of playing. That night I'd pretended to be asleep when I heard him coming upstairs, hoping that might prevent him from coming in to kiss me.

How had writing successfully carried me back to that night sixty years earlier? What did the dream itself say? I answered these questions superficially then: successful writing excited me like Father had; successful writing might also seem like a baby ready to come out. Both had scared me. More complete answers came years later after many more dreams.

Example #30

July 16, 1999

Writing industriously and with sustained effort, I now had the novel reorganized and the characters more developed in a book that was three chapters longer than before. But looking at the writing itself, especially in the new parts, I found the characters presented too superficially and the language too pedantic; it was boring and cognitive rather than moving. I'd done too little SHOWING. My images also seemed stunted and contrived, rather than full and natural. In short, the whole project felt too confined, as though my efforts to do it the "right" way had made the writing "weak." I decided the characters needed further development throughout.

When I pondered these criticisms, it occurred to me that this superficiality might be the result of myself clinging to the outside, unconsciously, that is, trying to not be aware of feelings myself because of terror about my own vulnerability if I left my parents behind to WRITE FOR MYSELF. Thus, in a way, my advances in writing had scared me back into the "suitcase." Also, the current point of view and verb tense problems I was struggling with could be ways of "protecting" myself from feeling like a "REAL WRITER." On the basis of this I decided that I needed to disobey the rules (mine and my parents') that had kept me in the suitcase. Those rules had been avoiding exhilaration, not connecting myself to the author of *Caleb, My Son*, and using "bored" for protection (see July 12, 1992 dream). Then I dreamed:

> I went to the Caswell Street house in the middle of the night with two rolled up newspapers. I went in the gate and up the front walk in the dark. At the front door lights went on inside. Scared, I put down the newspapers on the porch and left, surprised at not being attacked.
>
> I was climbing up into a house (like my beach house) through a system of connecting laundry chutes (like from the washer into the wall up to a bin inside). I was carrying small stuff that I had to put down on the edge. I was afraid the whole time as I moved from outer chute to inner chute that the alarm would go off. I could hear its slight beeping noise (that it makes when it's put on and gives you time to get out of the house before it's fully activated). I *did* get in *with* my stuff. This dream was initiated by me entering the garage and heading for the chute while Nancy Tilly, a seminar participant who was a considerable distance behind, called out to me and I ignored her.
>
> In a small class being taught by George Vaillant, I sat at the end of a table opposite him. He was talking about people with odd names and their theories.

When I couldn't understand the name of the person, I asked Vaillant to spell it and he did.

My colleague Heather called me up after I had had a difficult struggle (as with the laundry chutes) with a girl patient (maybe my former adolescent patient Josie?), to say that the girl had told her two things about this. One I don't remember but the other was that the girl had bitten my hand. I *knew* both of these were untrue and told Heather. But then I saw a red mark on the back of my right fist, like a tooth *had* pressed against it but not broken the skin.

Dream Aftermath

It is not surprising that I would have dreams about my beach house. Rudy and I had built it together, and later I felt very lonely there without him.

Here the efforts to climb into the beach house reminded me of the tube-feeding process I'd endured for months at New York Hospital. This led me to realize that besides the confining "suitcase" rules, I might also be kept away from my novel's inner richness by angry feelings about forced entry associated, among other things, with my having had to comply with the tube feedings. Thus, in more than one way, anorectic me was hurting my writing. "Fattening" this novel, which was the next step, would require not only confronting warm, charming, cruel Father but opposing my parents' and my own DO NOT ENTER rules. But also, out of the "suitcase," I might well have to feel and struggle with new awareness of hurt and anger that the "suit case" had protected me from earlier.

Background:

This dream impresses me as a good example of how subtle meanings can add tremendous clarity to present-day life. For instance:

The Caswell Street house is the home of my childhood, where the newspapers my family published often did arrive rolled up. Here, it seemed to me, they were clubs for war!

The laundry chute did resemble the tube-feeding paraphernalia!

Nancy Tilly is a writer who once attended my seminar. George Vaillant is a respected clinician and writer about ego defenses. His book, Adaptation to Life, had meant a lot to me. But, besides both being writers, I thought their names (till or "not yet" and valiant) might be the reason for their presence in this dream.

Heather Craige is an analyst and a friend. The denial of hurt to my right hand and then discovering its injury by an adolescent girl (anorexic me?) fit with how I was

*learning about the things that hindered me. I could see Heather as therapist me look-
ing at the scars on my writing left by my anorexic conflicts and their consequences.*

Example #31

October 1, 1999

The longer I worked at writing, the more I thought about competing with and/or being in the company of other writers. Sometimes this depressed me because I felt unimportant as a writer. But the better my writing work went, the more I could consider the meaning of IMPORTANT AS A WRITER to myself. It would amount to feeling "loved" by parents I now understood had been incapable of love. Therefore, IMPORTANT AS A WRITER was no longer what I really wanted. What I wanted now was TO DELIGHT MYSELF with the writing and to do so in a way that would put me in touch with people. These thoughts made working hard easier and primed me to notice and enjoy breakthroughs as they came. This also allowed the writing to matter in its own right because I wasn't using it for self worth. Making that distinction, I wondered about being able to enjoy it as a friend, as I do my adult daughter.

> Going "home" with stuff (maybe rolling suitcase full of writing). I was walking along and getting ready to go upstairs (by first entering this white walled curving ramp-corridor entry that reminded me of some particular place). I saw the shadow of a man on the inside wall of that ramp-entry. It scared me (like when I see a big loose dog when I'm walking Moonshine, my miniature dachshund) and I decided to go another way. Maybe that blocked me from the elevator at this lowest level. But I went to the elevator at the next highest level and discovered that it was hanging between floors. I could step down into it because it was an open seat, and I proceeded to get in. It was an odd open elevator made of mahogany or other dark polished wood and quite small. Just big enough for one person. It consisted of a seat on one side and foot holes opposite it like in a baby's swing.

Dream Aftermath

Elevators, I'd learned earlier, are mainly related to "up and down" feelings, especially involving self-esteem. This one, being open and small, seemed to connect with both my writing and my self-image. In keeping with that idea, this dream helped me to look at what else might happen if I gave up needing to be important as a writer and sought, instead, to produce writing that delighted me. Because I would no longer be clinging to unavailable parental "love," I might instead be able to utilize what my parents and their examples *had* offered me—Mommy's (unbearable and narcissistic) glowing praise and Father's warm, charming, and cruel way with words. My decision to avail myself of these qualities in them had likely created the small elevator in the dream—a way to rise to greater heights (in value) without getting FAT. I also realized from this, that for me, feeling really good about my voice and my writing could feel as out of control and as overwhelmed as being attacked by Father or praised mercilessly by Mommy.

Example #32

May 21, 2000

As I kept writing and revising the novel, it became clearer and clearer that I needed to feel adequate and write free of the old deforming rules if my product was to succeed. Simply put: I needed to stop deforming myself (by staying small and "perfect" and need-free) and my writing in order to please and stay with my parents. At the same time, when I went against the rules and felt STRONG from doing so, guilt from feeling WRONG followed instantly. The next task was to keep this from stopping me.

> Something about a toddler who talked easily…Then I was talking to a black woman sitting up and eating in a hospital bed. Her head, chin and neck were bandaged with just her face (eyes, nose, mouth, etc.) free. I felt I should have asked about her operation but didn't. She was eating out of plastic containers with lids. One of the containers held something red (like red soup or tomatoes). She put the lids on as she talked to me, saying, *"What scares me is that the other food they have is so good."*

Dream Aftermath

I decided that "putting the lid on" had to do with my being afraid to love or feel strongly about anything, including my writing and making contact with people. Wondering if this was because I feared behaving the way my parents had with other people, I reminded myself that despite being shy and having spent five years in mental hospitals, I had a far greater capacity to relate genuinely with people than either Mommy or Father. Remembering to feel proud about that would be another way of separating from them. Then I realized that the lid itself might represent the depression I often experienced when the writing went well. So it wasn't just that no longer being a crippled writer was a loss. I was *afraid* of any strong feelings.

Example #33

<u>October 9, 2000</u>

At this point, in addition to working consistently and effectively, I began to reach for new solutions in dealing with writing inside myself. Since I'd realized that writing with interruptions might be a way of suppressing my power and avoiding discovering something new and valuable, I resolved to keep myself driven in the writing process. Yet, doing this, I felt absolutely terrible! Then I concluded: writing this story is very, very hard and may be impossible. Therefore I need to work very, very hard because the story requires it, *not* because I'm inadequate. As I proceeded, I realized that feeling inadequate earlier had prevented me from even trying to do the work needed to produce writing of substance. To write masterfully would require losing myself in the story and struggling within it to make the story work.

> I went into a New York restaurant, but had brought my usual fare with me, because I was leery about their food. The cook (a black woman a little like our Leanna in childhood) told me we were having soup for dinner, and I could see people eating it at their dining tables. The soup was red and thick. She told me that there was also the meat of this big bird. It was huge and weird looking, sort of like a cross between a dinosaur and a pokemon. It also looked like it had been cooked standing up. I thought I might try some, because she said it tasted like chicken…Then I was alone in New York in the night and preparing to drive back to Raleigh without a reservation for a place to sleep on the way. I felt an odd mixture of *scared* and *cozy*.

<u>Dream Aftermath</u>

This dream reminded me of my continued rigidity about eating. It seemed to demonstrate that I was as afraid of my more adventurous fiction writing as I was of exotic foods. The red soup reminded me of the dish I'd put the lid on in my May 21, 2000 dream where I was wrapped in bandages. The big bird looked like something out of Pokemon land and reminded me of my feelings of weirdness as an anorexic and later as a former mental patient. I also decided that Pokemon represented the way I felt alone as a person and as a writer in the world of other people. I decided that the mixed feelings—scared and cozy—at the prospect of driving home alone in the night, had to do with driving to my death, driving to where my writing would be fully satisfying, and driving to where I'd encounter Father as attacker, seducer, and comforter.

Example #34

October 23, 2000

I had a whole day to write. Reviewing the novel before I continued, I realized that I'd accomplished a tremendous amount of work in it—good, imaginative writing. As a result, even though I *felt* wimpy and discouraged about myself as a writer, I really had no alternative but to write with a BIG VOICE. I had also recently hired another writer to read part of the book.

> I went back to New York Hospital for a Saturday morning appointment. But when I got there, it was dark and complex (like it really was and like these big hotels I keep dreaming about). My appointment was on the 4th floor. But when I got inside, I realized I no longer had the necessary key or remembered the route to get there. So I went to a desk to ask the receptionist for help.

Dream Aftermath

Perhaps I had gone back to New York Hospital now because that was where I'd written my first novel, *Caleb, My Son*, which had first brought me recognition as a writer. A Saturday morning appointment would have been odd at New York Hospital unless you were an inpatient. But Saturdays now were when I had the most time to write. My most important and terrifying appointment in the hospital had been with Dr. Burdick when she told me that I did not belong there and would need to prepare to leave. So why had I lost the key? And what was the "craziness" that would have kept me in the hospital? I decided that it must be the belief *that I could not write and was not a writer.* Two other thoughts followed: (a) "not being able to write" or "not being able to find the words" seemed similar to the terrible feeling of "LOST" I sometimes experienced at parties I went to alone; (b) hiding my writing behind craziness was like Father's hiding his glasses of Bourbon behind books when Grandfather came to visit.

Example #35

March 4, 2001

Shock and extreme sadness characterized the days preceding this dream. On February 25th, my beloved sister Bibba (while traveling back from Alaska where she'd been conducting workshops and readings in relation to her mystery series about a forgetful sleuth named Peaches Dam) had developed a strange skin infection. Within 24 hours she was dead! Bibba had been my lifelong hero. I'd talked in analysis about her possibly being another writer I wanted to preserve by staying small myself. Attending her memorial service with our extended family, I thought a lot about our different positions in the family and the lifelong consequences of those differences. As the first few days following Bibba's death passed, however, I also realized that this terrible tragedy was making me aware of things I would otherwise never have faced or realized.

Interestingly, too, though I had been thinking about needing to terminate my analysis with Dr. H. once this novel was completed, Bibba's death was followed by several dreams about *his* leaving me.

> I was at Dr. H.'s, lying down talking. (I was seeing myself do this from the front and side, maybe in a larger space, more like his old office, before the fire.) He was very quiet (like he *has* been lately), but I kept on talking. Then all these cleaning people were clearing out the place with me still lying on the couch. Only then did I realize Dr. H. was gone without saying good-bye, that it was the end of the session and he would see me next time.

Dream Aftermath

This was, in fact, a time frought with major losses. Besides Bibba's shocking and untimely death, Cleves, who was 62 and had been my beloved Oedipal baby, had undergone surgery for breast cancer 18 months earlier. Less than three weeks after Bibba's death, she came to Duke (from Hawaii) for surgery because of metastasis to her optic nerve. At this time, also, on the advice of several advisors, I was preparing my memoir for publication through the services of a private publisher. This last fact, alone, could have accounted for my loss of Dr. H. in dreams.

Example #36

April 3, 2001

By now, preparing speeches had become relatively easy, though still time-consuming. In contrast, I always dreaded work on the novel but felt at home once I got into it. I also noticed that when writing, I enjoyed it but feared losing myself. More thoughts along this line led me to consider that I'd never had a close relationship in which I could truly depend on the other person. You can only *depend* and find out whether the other is dependable if you are free to be your real self in their presence.

> I was at a big dinner meeting of our advisory council. It was held low down—as in elegant underground quarters. After dinner we went around to different displays to pick up favors. The ones I picked up were miniature—a silver dollhouse size roast chicken, a platter for it, lots of tiny brightly colored fabric bowls. Then I went back to my suitcase which was full and wide open on a rack in the corner beside David Finn's office. (So we were at Ruder-Finn, a public relations agency where David Finn was director.) But it had disappeared. I thought someone had knocked it down, and now I can't recall what happened…my daughter Lucy was in this dream, too…after that, I and others were trying to cross a major highway, Blue Ridge Road. But to do so we had to go through this large messy business (at the location where Polk Youth Camp used to be, which has now been taken over by the North Carolina Museum of Art). Maybe this business manufactured sludge or some concrete product in a big way. Its intricate space made it hard to find a place to go out and cross the highway. I tried a couple of times before I was about to get through at the end.

Dream Aftermath

If my large open suitcase was missing, it could be that I no longer needed it. I thought about the July 12, 1992 dream when I'd given up my little roller suitcase and felt naked and scrunched up (as if still in it) on Dr. H.'s floor. A lot had happened since then in both my life and my dream growth. That July 1992 dream had preceded my decision to convert my autobiographical novel into a memoir. Now probably that open suitcase (near David Finn's office) represented the memoir completed and no longer needing me. I suspected that the messy sludge production business I had to find my way through to get out to the highway represented the hard work still needed on the novel before I could get to the "high" way. I would need to feel "high" as a writer before I could get my "license to drive." Only days later did I remember that Blue Ridge Road was the location of both the NC Museum of Art and the Polk Youth Center, a facility for incarceration of young criminals. At the time the Art Museum was negotiating to take over the Youth Center land. Maybe, too, this dream reflected how laboring my way through the novel would involve letting the incarcerated youth (in me) be taken over by or converted to grand creativity or art. That might amount to letting myself feel as BIG and FINE as other people (including Mommy) seemed to think I was. Only several weeks later did it occur to me that the NC Department of Motor Vehicles office where I typically went for renewal of my driver's license was also located on Blue Ridge Road opposite the Youth Center.

Example #37

April 21, 2001

In the midst of preparations for the memoir's publication (including decisions and proof-reading on my part), I continued work on the novel. My effort at this juncture was to find and use my own way with words. I understood two things about this. When things were going well, the writing itself gave me a glow! That didn't happen often, but when it did, I knew it meant I was IN MY WRITING ROOM and competing with Father. Dr. H. had repeatedly said that what was needed for me to be the writer I wanted to be was to reject Father (sexually) and join him (professionally). Keeping ideas like this in mind made me think about how important Dr. H. was to me and how it would make me sad to terminate my work with him once the novel was completed.

> I was at this place that had back windows with rain outside (like at my daughter Lucy's house in the alcove leading to the backyard). I looked out more than once. Then, walking in the opposite direction, I entered the lobby of a hospital. There I bumped into Dee Haizlip whom I hadn't seen for years. She was carrying Little Tom, who looked to be about Lucy's Will's age (three). And they had a school writing paper of Tom's that looked precociously done. I had (or remembered) one of my son Ben's that was much less skilled. Talking to Dee, I learned that Big Tom was in critical condition in the hospital with everything (all the drugs and procedures) going wrong. He'd been shot while hunting. I felt guilty for not having seen the Haizlips for so long and for the bad things happening to such good and capable people without my helping them.

Dream Aftermath

This dream, along with current dealings with my children, prompted me to look back sadly and regretfully at how I'd been as a mother—a woman so painfully caught up with trying to make herself adequate as woman, wife, and mother that she'd been unable to devote herself fully to her children despite giving up writing. I saw little Tom in the dream as myself and big Tom as my father. The whole dream reminded me of a TAT (Thematic Apperception Test, a projective test sometimes used in psychological evaluations) card which deals with a son's feelings about his father's being close to death. At this time I was on my way to speak at a national conference of psychologists, and it occurred to me, in the process, that both anorexia and my career as a psychologist had been ways of straining to not be a writer and, therefore, to *not* kill Father. Of course, such straining and reaction formation would be the cover for strong negative feelings.

Background:

   Tom and Dee Haizlip were good and helpful friends from the period of raising small children and later from the early years of my divorce. The fact that in their family father and son had the same name, Tom, which was also the name of my first husband, was a similarity with my family where there were five generations of Lucy's.

Example #38

July 27, 2001

At this time I was involved in many business details related to publishing *With a Woman's Voice* and putting my two novels back into print. The LDF also continued making demands on me. When I read the obituaries of Eudora Welty, whom I'd known slightly, I felt a mixture of failure, intimidation, and disappointment related to my wish to be a writer. But I also felt enviously inspired to write like Eudora. That is: I wanted to write *as myself* and out of what *I* knew personally just as she had.

> I was riding in a taxi with all my stuff—several things besides a pocketbook that I had to carry. I got out of the cab, careful to take all my stuff with me, and the cab drove away. *Only then did I realize that I had left the shopping bag holding all my writing in the cab. I felt devastated.*

Dream Aftermath

First I thought of this dream as defensive—a way to stop feeling afraid and guilty about becoming a writer. Then I wondered if it was about the loss of the writing to the power of the story. Had I, the RIDER (writer) lost my writing to the DRIVER (its power)? Though I assumed this was related to the impending publication of my memoir, in life I kept working hard on the novel.

Example #39

August 1, 2001

As I prepared for a seminar I would teach in the spring and continued work on the novel, I thought, what does it mean to insist that *I am not a writer*? Was I saying, "I am 'good' and 'small' and, therefore, 'safe' from Father's jealousy" or "I *refuse* to grow up and be the writer you want me to be"? Then I thought: writing while not claiming myself as a writer is like staying a "greasy grind" who doesn't grow up. And calling myself a "greasy grind" instead of a writer, again, amounted to hiding my books behind craziness the way Father had hidden his Bourbon behind the books!

> I went to Holly Peppe's house. Dottie Jeffries was there. At one point I was walking along behind them as Holly, at least, carried a big box of something (papers, I thought). Both Holly and Dottie looked younger than they are. Holly's house was not her New York apartment (which I've never visited) but more like the house Tom and I lived in on Rogerson Drive (when Pat was born, where I began *High on a Hill*)...I went into the bathroom. The toilet paper holders were like electric sockets or the electric sockets were toilet paper holders. By this I mean, when I tried to pull off some toilet paper to clean up some dropped grains of instant coffee, I could only get one square, because it snapped back in...I did drop instant coffee beside the commode and wanted to clean it up so Holly wouldn't know. I dropped it, because I didn't want it anymore or felt I shouldn't have it. I did get most of it picked up in that single square of toilet paper, however...At one point I was sitting talking to Dottie and Holly.

Dream Aftermath

Holly Peppe and Dottie Jeffries are both professional writers. Following behind them and then going into the bathroom instead of staying in their presence seemed to represent me following in their footsteps as a real writer but again succumbing to humiliation at the prospect. The Rogerson Drive house was where I'd worked as a professional writer and Guggenheim fellow in literature (publishing a short story and an article, "Black Out in Prince Edward" about one Virginia community's defiance of integration, for Coronet Magazine, as well as working on *High on a Hill*) before college and where I had my first baby. When I looked at the dropped instant coffee and the single squares of toilet paper I got because the electric toilet paper holders snapped at me, I thought about keeping my writing small. In analysis I talked with Dr. H. about how proud Father had been of

Caleb, My Son and about how—when he kept saying "You *are* a writer" long after I'd stopped—I'd told myself, "No, I'm not." When Dr. H. said, "In the sense, 'And you can't make me!'?", I agreed. The instant coffee, I decided after much thought, was my way, in waking life, of trying to get empowered from outside to compensate for having to feel inadequate inside.

Example #40

August 29, 2001

I felt depressed for a few days and I couldn't understand why, except that I also felt very alone as I awaited the publication of *With a Woman's Voice*. I dreamed:

> Vivid bit of dream. In it I felt miserable about going through my whole life as a weak and inadequate writer. The misery had to do with having to go all the way to old age feeling insufficient while still writing.

Dream Aftermath

I decided that one reason for a dream like this at this time (in keeping with my present depression) might be to reassure my unconscious that my memoir and especially the novel would not turn me into a REAL and SUCCESSFUL WRITER.

Example #41

August 30, 2001

I continued work on the novel despite my depression, which still seemed unrelated.

A long and terrifying nightmare. Now I can only summarize it:

> I went to a house for shelter during a bombing like the London blitz. Our friends and neighbors—even some in that house—were against us. The bombs falling all around were about to hit this house. We were trying to get into a low down place for shelter. But the people in the house wouldn't share them. They wanted us to leave or die in this war zone.

Dream Aftermath

I could not immediately understand this dream. Instead I began to notice how I was missing Rudy, my second husband. I missed the glow I'd felt with him and with Father. Rudy had been very controlling, however, and confining. Missing him made me remember how from very early in life—since I'd climbed into a bureau drawer to sleep after my younger sister's birth—I had associated being cribbed with being cared for. Maybe that was another reason I'd been so "good" in the yard. Maybe I was missing that confinement now as I experienced increased freedom.

I began to think of the dreams from the two previous nights as representing my whole writing dilemma. Whereas I hated going to my grave feeling like a worthless and inadequate writer, not staying an inadequate writer would make me feel like an unwilling but trapped suicide bomber—destroying the world with my power and not even being able to save myself in the process.

Example #42

September 6, 2001

Continuing work on the novel while anticipating early copies of the memoir, I counseled myself that in terms of both writing and death, this was a time for courage. Because I really was going to die (as both an aging alive person and a non-writer) and I really did want to be a writer. All my life I'd been controlled unconsciously by the fantasy of being the dead woman Father could love. My April 1989 dream had portrayed this deadness as the white goodness all over my body. Now I was about to give that up.

> A very important dream which I can't fully remember. What little I do recall has to do with a mixture of sadness and victory or sadness and excitement. I was talking earnestly with this blonde long-haired young man (whom I tried to treat years ago) who exposed himself sexually to little girls. I was telling him good-bye while feeling sad and victorious.

Dream Aftermath

This is the 45th anniversary of the publication of *Caleb, My Son.*

This dream showed me saying goodbye, with a mixture of sadness and victorious pleasure, to a "beloved" child molester. He, like the pedophile in my July 12, 1992 dream, resembled a young man I had tried to treat early in my career as a psychologist. I believed he represented my feelings about needing to take care of my sexually abusive father. And now, with a memoir and a novel I might be at a place of saying, "I cannot and will not take care of Father." Maybe, too, this allowed my first realization that taking care of Father by not claiming my own power was like complying with sexual abuse.

Example #43

November 19, 2001

Still feeling quite isolated as I worked on the novel and awaited advance copies of the memoir, I dreamed:

> I was at a conference site that reminds me of the sterile, ultramodern house I went to Thursday night. While there I realized I needed to cut off my hand. But I was afraid to. I went upstairs to get these doctors (including a tall, slim, dark-haired one I associated with LDCEC Director Don Rosenblitt) to help me. I had a huge butcher knife and went over to a table and tried to do it. I got so close to succeeding that I could feel the cut on my wrist all the way around. But I was too afraid. So then these doctors were going to help me. I lay down for this doctor to do it. But I was still terribly afraid. I kept telling myself not to be afraid and it was the right thing to do. But I *was* afraid that cutting off my hand would kill me. This doctor, who looked like the new editor in my October 27, 2001 dream, was preparing to do it. But suddenly he got called away (perhaps to the Afghan war).

Dream Aftermath

Immediately after this vivid dream I felt baffled. Of course I knew that, as always, the hand had to do with my writing. I'd been afraid in the dream that cutting off my hand would cause me to cease to exist, though at the same time I thought it needed to be cut off. I remembered that I believed that architect W.G. Clark's having been born with only one hand had contributed to the beauty of his buildings, including the one he designed for the Lucy Daniels Foundation. I assumed that cutting off my hand was like cutting off my writing, *really* making me a *non-writer*. Only several days later did it occur to me that the hand I'd wanted cut off in the dream had been my left hand, my *non-writing* hand. So, what I'd dreamed about without realizing it at first had been *no longer existing as a non-writer!*

Background:

Donald Rosenblitt is a nationally respected psychiatrist and psychoanalyst who serves as medical director of the Lucy Daniels Center for Early Childhood. Besides being a friend and colleague, his kind and astute work with children may have been the inspiration for his role in this dream.

Example #44

<u>April 2, 2002</u>

Though work on the novel continued, other events became more pressing. The LDF and the LDCEC were planning a conference, "The Artist as Child," in New York on April 25th. My memoir's publication date was April 15th. I was scheduled to go to New York early and spend a few days with Jonathan and his wife, Sonja. Anticipating all this, I dreamed:

> I discovered that I had lost Moonshine's leash. This was accompanied by despair and a strong sense of loss.

<u>Dream Aftermath</u>

I considered walking Moonshine, whom I loved dearly, a conscientious duty. As a dachshund, however, she was, of course, an "under dog" like I'd felt much of my life. Probably this dream had to do with my feelings about losing myself as an "under dog" on Mommy's leash. If I was no longer tied to her with this leash and, therefore, no longer an "under dog" (boy writer), then I had a chance to be a woman who spoke and wrote for herself. My existence would no longer have to be limited to copying and not overshadowing Father.

I realized, too, that a small eating binge the week before had resembled the desperation of the repeated eating binges I'd had right after leaving the hospital. All had been triggered by the terror of losing myself as the underdog.

Example #45

<u>April 24, 2002</u>

In New York for several days prior to our conference on "The Artist as Child," I felt remarkably adequate and at ease. I was doing unusual things—seeing publicists and advisors as well as potential donors to the Lucy Daniels Foundation. I had also already received recognition and appreciation from several people who'd read the memoir. Yet the book had not been reviewed by any newspaper and I suspected would not be. I had also enjoyed my time in New York with Jonathan and Sonja who were expecting their first child. The day before this one, I'd felt exceptionally at home and experienced, capable and acceptable at a higher status with a mix of people in this city I still associated with parental visits during my hospitalization.

> This was not a dream, but its vividness on the morning of April 24th reminds me of a dream. When I woke that morning I was *terrified.* This terror was similar to that during eating binges after the hospital, only much, much worse. I felt driven to jump off a cliff despite the terror of doing so.

<u>Dream Aftermath</u>

I was able to understand on my own that the earlier eating binges and "too much" of various things had been my unconscious' way of warding off this terror. "Too much" always put me "down" with guilt after experiences (like the day before) which made me feel worthy, accepted, belonging, and capable. At least now, it seemed, I must feel strong enough to face this TERROR and have a chance to understand it.

In a telephone session later that morning, Dr. H. had something else very valuable to say: "The one thing children fear worse than abandonment in families like yours is being overwhelmed and swallowed up by their parents. You fended this off with both of yours."

Example #46

<u>May 24, 2002</u>

Now that *With a Woman's Voice* was in circulation, I received a flood of positive reactions to it. Lucy and her husband Billy gave me a party to celebrate the publication. I received numerous letters from a variety of strangers. I was interviewed on radio and television and gave readings at bookstores. The upshot, of course, was that I was out in the world and recognized as a writer. I began to realize that "Not good enough" had been a way to hide both my writing and myself. And hiding like that had kept me from knowing how good a writer I could be. I decided I did need to keep showing myself to see what I could learn or gain from doing so. But there were still no reviews.

Thinking about aging and death, I walked through my house and remembered how my father had denied me the money to buy it and criticized me as "selfish and greedy" even to want a house in town. This enabled me for the first time to fully recognize Father's cruelty to me. I realized in the process, however, that I still could not feel angry toward him about this even though I *had* stood up to him when he ridiculed my desire to live in town. Then I dreamed:

> I was driving somewhere at a distance from and south of Raleigh, maybe toward Hilton Head (where my parents lived in their later years) in an open convertible. The highway's name was a two-digit number like 85. I came to a place where it seemed I should take a detour to the right (to get where I was going more quickly). But when I did, I ended up in Grandfather's formal garden where proceeding would mean jumping down (in the car) these steps to a lower garden level where there was no highway. So I turned around to go back to the main highway. But I was running things by a hand-held gadget (like a remote control) and had trouble remembering how to distinguish the numbers for speed from those for highway or the direction for veering the car and its tires. I somehow got back on a main road and was going somewhere for a purpose, maybe to pick up a young girl.
>
> I ended up in downtown Raleigh, going on a one-way street past where I needed to go. I had to drive around the block to come back to my destination. Once there, I was *way* high up on a platform and would need to get down from it onto the main road in a huge open elevator. In the place of turning back around or near driving onto the lift, there seemed to be a yucky bug flying loose (but hard to catch) in the car. Then, when it was still, these ladies on the outside discovered it was really a little animal. I was terrified of the extreme height of the elevator, but the women running the garage seemed to expect me to go along with business as usual. I drove the car right up to the edge like they told me to. Then the bottom dropped out and the car *fell* to the

lower level! Three stories maybe! No one was hurt; nor was the car damaged. But it *was* *terrifying!*

Dream Aftermath

Surprised that the huge fall in the dream had not hurt me or damaged the car, I understood, with Dr. H.'s help, that this dream had to do with my devaluing Father. A new question followed: Why had I valued him so highly? Partly because everything he'd said had sounded so real and strong even when it was cruel and inappropriate. I also realized that I might have valued him highly to have *some* value myself. But while putting myself down with the anger he caused me had preserved the possibility of my being loved by a real person, I'd also always felt worthless in relation to both Father's cruelty and my need to feel safe from his "love."

Example #47

Summer 2002

Summer 2002 proved to be transformational in more than one way. In June, everyone in and around Raleigh seemed to know about my memoir. Calls came in asking me to do readings in cities throughout North Carolina. The *News &* *Observer*, formerly our family's newspaper, called to set up an interview and photo requests early in June. Then they published a full page and a half feature on me and a critical review of the book on Sunday, June 23rd. There was widespread response to this feature including a scathing letter to the editor from my first husband and fan letters from people who knew me through the LDF. I felt warmed by the general response, but of course, I talked at length with Dr. H. about my mix of thrill and distress.

July 1, 2002

Then on the morning of July 1st, Dr. H.'s wife called to cancel his session with me that day. The odd thing about this cancellation, which she left on my voice mail at work, was that Dr. H. did not make it himself and there was no mention of subsequent sessions. At first I worried that Dr. H. had been injured in a motorcycle accident I'd heard about on the radio and television. But then I realized that the people in that accident had been chased by the highway patrol, and I knew that Dr. H. would not have participated in that. At the end of the day I had two more messages from his wife. The first said that Dr. H.'s aorta had collapsed and he was recovering from the surgery to repair it. In the second, she asked me to call her at home. From her tone of voice, I knew even before speaking with her that Dr. H. had died. I have no words to describe the shock and grief that followed. The person I depended on most in life had disappeared.

July 4, 2002

I dreamed:

> My right arm had been ripped off at the shoulder. I was not terrified (as in the November 18, 2002 dream) or in anguish. It was just savagely gone.

Dream Aftermath

I felt painfully alone and abandoned without Dr. H. Then I noticed that in writing about this brutal blow in my copybook, I had written Dr. H.'s "birth" rather than "death." Pondering this mix-up, I wondered: Could it possibly be that Dr. H.'s death was for me both the loss of a vital part of myself *and* a birth within me? For instance, could this terrible blow help me lose Father's remaining importance in me so that I and my power could flourish more freely? The fact that dear wise Dr. H., who had been there for me for twenty-seven years, had suddenly been taken away made me think of losing him as a narcissistic self-object, a felt part of myself. The July 4th dream was an apt expression of that. Putting that dream together with what Dr. H. had said to me about other losses in the course of my long analysis—"this is very sad and painful but it is also an opportunity to grow"—I could think of my ripped-off right arm as leaving a gap for me to grow a new one. And, of course, I do write with my right hand. I knew, too, because of all the losses of destructive relationships I had had to work through previously, that this was my first loss of a good object—one I did not have to worry about identifying with or copying unconsciously.

Attending the memorial service, I had other insights that would never have been available to me had Dr. H. lived. In my experience of him as both analyst and respected medical director of the Wake County Alcoholism Treatment Center, he had always had a ponytail and worn cowboy boots and denim pants. I knew that besides driving an SUV he rode a motorcycle; I'd seen the motorcycle trailer, with its "hawg dawg" license plate, on which his border collie McTavish rode after him. But I learned from the photographs at the service—packed to standing room only with all kinds of people, including thirty or so Harley Davidson motorcyclists—that as a young groom he had been short-haired and preppy looking. From this I recognized Dr. H. as a role model as well as a good object (an internalized experience with a good-enough caretaker). In his office he had devoted himself to listening and judiciously responding to someone like me. Outside his office he'd lived life to the hilt for himself.

Example #48

July 27, 2002

I continued doing readings of my memoir and working on the novel. I deliberately kept my former analytic hours free to help myself experience rather than deny this huge loss and my reactions to it. Then one night at the beach house alone with Moonshine I dreamed:

> I was taking a course that I hadn't studied for and we were to have the exam in a week or 10 days. But besides that, although I had my PhD, there was at least one *major* undergraduate course that I never had completed. I had the idea of putting both these tests together and getting permission to not take the current test the next week, but rather to take both tests in the fall so that I could use the whole summer to study for both. I talked to someone about this—someone like a husband—and they didn't think it was such a good idea. They thought it would just keep me a drudge and greasy grind all summer, robbed of *that* pleasure in the service of anxiety.
>
> Also, at one point, I was in a *dark*, mostly empty movie theater, sitting in a row with space in front of it. In the dark, I noticed some small shiny things on the floor. Picking them up, I realized they were earrings (two pairs for pierced ears). I believe that a young woman (maybe me when I got my PhD) then came up and claimed one pair.

Dream Aftermath

Because the neglected course or test had not prevented me from getting my PhD, I decided that test must be the writing I still needed to do now. Then it occurred to me that the *real* test might be *showing* myself—as Dr. H. had always shown himself—*quietly*. In the dream the MOVIE (a place that moves you) theater had been dark and empty. Maybe because Dr. H. was no longer showing. The earrings would be the voices that still rang in my ears. Perhaps Father's and Dr. H.'s. They had both told me I was indeed a writer.

Example #49

September 26, 2002

The summer of 2002 was packed with activities associated with the publication of *With a Woman's Voice*. But as busy as I was, I religiously continued work on the novel. I was surprised and gratified at how effectively I went about my life despite the painful loss of Dr. H. But then, as my aloneness swelled large, I pondered the effects of Dr. H.'s death on me and my writing. With numerous other demands, both personal and at the LDF, I decided to seek consultation from an analyst in New York. The night before doing so, I dreamed:

> As the dream began, it was like I was in analysis with Dr. H. sitting behind me. But instead of the reclining chair of recent years or the chaise lounge before that, I was lying on the somewhat lumpy mattress of the single bed in the tiny room that became my bedroom after Adelaide was born when I was about 27 months old. Behind me, Dr. H. (as a cadaver) was speaking. I don't remember the few carefully chosen words, but the gist of them was to ease me into talking about death, not my feelings about the transition of death itself but about *my* thoughts about *his* feelings about dying and being dead…After a while I noticed there were several other people in this tiny room (where I had slept alone and, out of fear, pretended to be asleep at age four when my baby sister was born and I was alone in the house with Father)…Then Dr. H. and I shifted our positions so that we were sitting close together side by side, sideways on the bed and with our backs against the wall beside it. In that position I could see Dr. H.'s large right hand very close to me. By then everybody had left except my cousin Edgar. While I was looking at Dr. H.'s hand, Edgar stood in front of us, leaned over and kissed Dr. H. good-bye on the mouth and left, too. This emphasized that it was a good-bye, parting situation. Focusing on Dr. H.'s cadaverous hand, I could see that it was strong but stiff and hardened and leathery. At times I wondered whether it was really his hand or a boxing glove. I decided it was both, a mix.

Dream Aftermath

I realized right away what a remarkable gift this dream was. Dr. H.'s different positions in it as well as the prominence of his right arm later in the dream told me fairly quickly that this was an imaging of what Dr. H. had told me several times—that to be a writer, I needed to reject Father and join him. Other features stood out dramatically: the room etched in my memory from my sister Cleves' birth and the earlier dream in it (March 31, 1999), and Edgar kissing Dr. H. goodbye on the mouth. I understood rather quickly (because of the bizarreness of this image) that Edgar (my cousin who'd been curly headed and fat ever since he was adopted at age three) represented "fat boy" me (the anorexic adolescent) kissing Father goodbye—an act I had hidden to save myself from at four because it terrified me. I understood, too, comparing this and the March 31, 1999 dream, that the room itself represented sexuality in its most primal form to me. Again the right arm, Dr. H.'s this time. I would need, I knew from all my years of work, to use the sexual power of that room to leave behind both Dr. H. and anorexic and inhibited-writer me.

Example #50

January 25, 2004

I was returning to Raleigh after a week in New York where I'd attended the meetings of the American Psychoanalytic Association. In the sixteen months between this date and the last dream presented here, I had written and dreamed copiously. In addition to revising the novel, I had prepared a major talk related to the LDF and my memoir that I'd presented in Atlanta and Los Angeles. In December of 2003, I'd spoken in a "Meet the Author" session at the national annual meeting of the American Academy of Psychoanalysis. Despite all this very successful functioning, I continued to have sad thoughts about Dr. H. and about how wasted he would have felt by the loss of his life.

In the airport on the way home, I pondered these sad Dr. H. thoughts that were so often in my head. This effort carried me back to the dreams on September 26, 2002 and July 27, 2002. Soon I realized that the September 2002 dream had been a reversal without appearing to be. In it I'd had Dr. H.'s voice putting *his* feelings into me. Perhaps this was because I *so* valued his voice that even though rationally I *knew* he was dead, emotionally I had to keep his voice alive. In the September 2002 dream, in fact, *though I had seen him with my eyes as a cadaver, my ears had heard his voice.* So in that dream I had used Dr. H. to do what Dr. H. would never have wanted me to do—instruct me to feel and stay preoccupied with the feelings of a corpse about dying and being dead.

This realization allowed the psychologist in me to come forward to my rescue. I realized that I had used empathy for Dr. H. as the defense mechanism of CONFUSION in order to avoid the pain of losing him. But, as is often true of defenses, this had actually caused me *more* pain, possibly by messing up my writing and by keeping the loss of Dr. H. current rather than worked through and done. In fact, what I'd been thinking about earlier there in the airport was the problem of mixing up voices of characters in a story I was writing and had discussed during my New York visit with a writer friend!

Yes, such a trick, while interesting and poignant, deprived me of some freedom. To really be free, I had to lose Dr. H. and focus on MY feelings—MY feelings about his loss, about myself, about my aloneness, and about my writing. Yes, accepting the emotional loss of Dr. H. and his voice was necessary for me to be able to use MY OWN VOICE most powerfully.

I also understood clearly that while Father had "loved" me as an "under dog," Dr. H. had not. Though I might have unconsciously believed he did, Dr. H. had recognized, applauded, and encouraged my strength, striving, and successes. He had only left me and everything else because he couldn't prevent doing so.

Example #51

June 5, 2004

In the months that followed, I continued to work hard on the novel, this time revising it after hearing responses from three different readers, one of whom was the editor I'd worked with on the memoir. In the past year I'd also used my experience in self-publishing *With a Woman's Voice* and re-printing my novels, along with horror stories from other writers about working with commercial presses, as I thought through my wishes about publishing this, my first novel in 43 years. I decided to make it as good as I could; seek the opinion and possibly the assistance of an agent; carefully examine the interest or offer of any commercial or academic press; and unless I was very satisfied with a commercial offer, publish the book on demand with a digital press. In keeping with this plan, once the novel was as good as I could see to make it, I sent it to Carl Brandt, my old agent, who'd expressed an interest in reading it. In the heat of these final preparations, I dreamed:

> I was with Moonshine in my house. Then my housekeeper, Lillian, took her to a vet appointment. My granddaughter Katherine was sitting on the stairs in my front hall, keeping the front door locked with a large key that she carried around. Then I was in my car driving up to the front of my house. Lillian came out the front door and told me Moonshine had died. I felt *awful*! *So shocked and grief-stricken I didn't know how I could go on!!*

Dream Aftermath

In the course of my frenzy to get this novel out, I had also been abusing myself with more coffee and wine than my stomach could tolerate. This dream let me know what huge, painful feelings of loss finishing the novel was causing me. And, as with recognizing my terror of losing myself in New York on April 24, 2002, I understood what a blessing it was to recognize these painful emotions and, therefore, no longer have to be deformed by straining to avoid them. Shock and grief at the prospect of losing myself as beloved "under dog" were feelings I *could* bear. And if I *could* send this novel off *and* not abuse myself physically, I would cease to be the "under dog" in two ways at once. This felt far more possible than at any time in the past because of my new feelings of independence in relation to writing and publishing.

Other Artists' Dream Clues

Another source of satisfaction for me has been the way people creating in a variety of media are able to make effective use of the two-mirror approach. While these dream efforts are frequently not as driven or symbol-focused as those required by my struggle to overcome writer's block, their versatility is awesome. My hope is that the entries included here will demonstrate this versatility and other unique strengths. Such variety in dream benefits allows me to believe that the two-mirror approach can be helpful in even more ways than I've imagined. I deeply appreciate these individuals' willingness to contribute their dream experiences to this book.

Harriet Hoover, 24-year-old North Carolina artist and designer

The Dreamer:

Harriet is an artist and fabric designer who recently graduated from the North Carolina State University College of Design and is planning to continue her career in Philadelphia. She grew up in a small western North Carolina town, the middle daughter of a butcher and a nurse who considered art and its manufacture a frivolous waste of time at best. This bit of down-to-earth irony is something Harriet talks about and expresses in her art.

Fall 2002
Background and Preface to the Dream:

This dream occurred when I was taking Lucy Daniels' class as a part of studying textile art at NC State University. I was beginning to move from working with textiles to making artwork with the earth and photographing decay. This change allowed me to conceptually focus on the brevity of human existence. In the process, I was coming to trust my work and myself as never before after a lifetime of shame and embarrassment, especially in making and exhibiting art that most people in my hometown could not understand. Another reason for my increased confidence was that I had just returned from a summer study in Central Europe.

The Dream

A dog greeted me at the beginning of a long pathway, almost a dirt road. This dog was big and hairy, the size and stature of a small horse. He could communicate without talking and directed me to ride on his back. The dog and I rode very fast down this dirt road; it was sunny and the air was crisp. Strong trees whipped by, their shadows rolling in repetition. We arrived at an art exhibition that was housed in a mental institution near my home. The art exhibition was highly publicized. We had to present our identification card and a small amount of cash to participate in the exhibition. The exhibition consisted of people being cast in dirt and mud, their mud shell being the complete work. The participants being cast in dirt treated it as a religious experience. Posters, displaying smiling faces exclaiming—"It's just like dying—you're going to love feeling new again!" were plastered to the walls. There were rows and rows of dirt shells to prove the exhibition's popularity. The dog and I were very afraid. I mounted his back and we rode away till we found a construction site to rest at.

Aftermath and Analysis of the Dream

I processed the dream by physically recreating it. While staging the dream and exploring the physical places keenly exposed in its landscape, I was able to develop a way of meditation through making art. The next day, I biked to the mental institution where the dream took place. The day was just as it had been in my dream, cool, early autumn air and sunny. I rode my bike down a very similar road with tremendous oaks lining both sides of it. My senses were heightened—it was a day when rainbows are transmitted through tears. I found an isolated field; I sat and began to collect the earth in my hands and made mud balls out of it. I made many of these and allowed them to dry at my house. Over several months, they became a meditative practice.

The presence of the mental institution was derived from my parents' pressure and paranoia surrounding the making of artwork throughout my youth. Sculpture and painting were methods of survival throughout my earliest adulthood. The work and its making have been associated with being "crazy" and depressed/possessed. I've often been forced to hide my paintings from my mother as she threatened to hospitalize me for their subject matter. The dream method of getting to the mental institution, via the dog's back, cleared me of any guilt or responsibility for attending the art exhibition. This aspect of the dream is an important representation of the solitude and peacefulness surrounding the making of the mudballs and finding the field. I was not ashamed or confused by the mudballs' natural occurrence, for I was not driving (responsible) in the dream. Upon arrival at the exhibition, I had to present my identification and money. This translates into my insecurities as an artist, concerning issues of identity and valid cultural background. Since I'd grown up in a blue-collar, working class family with very little money and no precedent for making art, which represented the elite and luxury, could I afford to enter the art exhibition in my dream? Was I a valid participant? Finally, the propaganda that surrounded the performance art of dirt casting was derived from my religious history. I fear the extreme anticipation and blind faith that surrounds groups with extreme beliefs. In the dream, this fear caused me to flee, without experiencing the "death and resurrection" through the exhibited artwork.

Kristen Dill, 48-year-old Raleigh, North Carolina painter

The Dreamer:

Kristen grew up in a family of artists. Both her parents paint, as did her maternal grandmother and great grandmother as well as her identical twin sister. Yet Kristen's parents consider themselves amateurs and were vociferous in their criticism when she majored in art in college. After college Kristen worked in graphic design until she was diagnosed with a chronic illness in her thirties. Then she began painting full-time, exhibiting and selling her work. Kristen is married and has a son in college.

October 2002
Background and Preface to the Dream:

I grew up one of three children in a creatively competitive family. After painting in watercolor for 12 years, my desire to work had become stale. In September I switched mediums to oil paint. This gave me new energy to go into the studio each morning. Painting felt like an adventure again rather than a well-worn path. I did have feelings of regret about turning my back on years of experience and sales as a watercolor artist.

The Dream

I am with my mother and sister sitting on the ground beside a lake. A beautiful white object appears and moves across the lake. We stare transfixed. What is it? Looks like glass or leaves falling and it flutters as it moves individual pieces. I move away from mother to try to see clearer. Too near her to take it in. It's a bird! We all three realize it's a DOVE! Gorgeous, exquisite, delicate, finely formed, perfect. It flies away from us.

A fish jumps out of the water and grabs it. "Oh no!" we all cry. "The fish is going to kill it." I think "No," and race around the lake hoping to save it. As I reach the bird, the dove has turned into a chicken and is pulled down a hole. I see its feet disappear down the hole. The fish has pulled the chicken down. I feel bad. The chicken pops up out of the hole. I reach for it and clasp it to my breast, relieved. I can't believe it. I thought it was a meal for the fish.

I cut off its head, turn it upside down to drain it.

Aftermath and Analysis of the Dream

I was fascinated by this dream with its strong symbols and contrast of saving the bird and then killing it.

My mother and sister are both artists. The three of us standing by a lake riveted on a visual object is something I associate with painting. This is because of the way we do stare, trying to make sense visually of what we're seeing.

In the dream, the move away from my mother to see more clearly reminds me of my psychological journey away from my engulfing mother. That shift was the first step in being able to paint freely.

The fish seems to symbolize the blocks to painting that rise out of my unconscious and take away my motivation to paint.

The dove turns into a chicken as I race to save it. The dove in the dream is delicate, fragile, and compared to glass at one point, while the chicken is plebian and seems about to become food as I cut off its head. As I thought about this contrast, it reminded me of the difference between waiting on inspiration to paint and showing up each day in my studio to get the work done. Although originally I was horrified at symbols that seemed to indicate I killed inspiration, the rare bird, as I worked with the symbols I began to understand that painting was no longer a rare, delicate experience for me. Rather it had become something I could race to pursue, track down, and hold in my hands. Truly possess. The act of cutting off the chicken's head came to seem like ownership and even confidence. Transforming a rarity into daily food.

After working with the dream, I moved forward with trying the new medium, embracing the challenges and growing in confidence. This dream also helped me stay aware of feelings of fragility that crop up as I paint. Exposing the desire for inspiration and the emotions that go with it enabled me to paint through those blocking emotions.

Sue Etheridge, 60-year-old North Carolina art therapist

The Dreamer:

Sue works as an art therapist both in private practice and at the Federal Prison at Butner, NC. Her job at the prison requires tremendous ingenuity because of the variety of extreme individuals incarcerated and hospitalized there. Sue's creativity showed itself long before she officially became an art therapist, however, as evidenced by this life-changing dream she reports from 1984.

Background and Preface to the Dream:

I was stuck. I had been enduring a loveless marriage to a fundamentalist minister for 18 years. This kept me essentially isolated, 1500 miles from my family of origin, living in near poverty in a rural town in northeastern North Carolina.

An important coping mechanism for me was that I cultivated for myself a local surrogate father—a humble man I met at work (I was bookkeeper in a car parts store and he was maintenance supervisor on a fleet of trucks in a local business). A generation older than me, he was an enormously supportive friend, the only one I had who was completely separate from church involvement. He had maintained my car for me so that I could complete my art degree as a commuting student. More importantly, he provided emotional undergirding that enabled me to survive through grueling circumstances in my marriage.

And now after 8 years he was dying of cancer. I felt like I was dying too.

The Dream

On the night before Thanksgiving I had this dream:

> The setting was the church parsonage where I lived. I was on the phone with Lucille—an annoying church member, who often called, monopolizing my time for hours of meaningless chit-chat. Suddenly, I recognized that my mother was there in the room. She said, "Look who's here." I turned and saw my Grandma Rogers. I tried to excuse myself from Lucille on the phone, but she just kept talking. My mother said, "Look who else is here." Then my Grandma Quinn, my favorite, appeared. I dropped the phone and ran into her arms. I could feel her rigid corset stays and flabby arms. I felt deeply comforted.

Aftermath of the Dream

I awoke with a feeling of euphoria after months of anticipatory grief. Although my grandmothers had been dead for many years and my mother was far away, they were present with me in the dream in vividly sensory ways. It was as though my unconscious had gone through its filing cabinet of all previous experiences, pulled out the perfect soothing moment, and gifted it to me in my dream. I had a new awareness of the permanence of important relationships in memory—even beyond death.

The next morning I was able to leave the obligatory frenzy of Thanksgiving cooking to go to the hospital and whisper to my friend as he slept that all was complete and it was all right with me to let go. It seemed his coma deepened and his suffering diminished. I took my turn sitting with him over the weekend. Much of that time I made drawings of my dying helper. Early Tuesday morning he slipped away.

This experience left me with confidence in the unconscious as a protecting and comforting force, accessible in dreams and having the capacity to lead to emotional strength.

Greg Lindquist, 25-year-old NC artist and writer

The Dreamer:

Greg is a recent graduate in literature and art and design from North Carolina State University. His interest in both areas began ten years ago in high school when he sought to relate helpfully with his father who had been diagnosed with cancer. Greg's father died in 2002, but Greg has continued his art and story creating efforts through his undergraduate career and more recently as a public school teacher. The dream he reports occurred as he was about to begin graduate study at Pratt Institute in New York.

July 19, 2004
Background and Preface to the Dream:

In preparation for my first move out of North Carolina, where I have lived until the age of twenty-five, I put my car up for sale. After selling my car in a bank parking lot to a guy from Bulgaria who mistook me for a Czech, I slept the afternoon away.

The Dream

I am in my former professor and her husband's kitchen, which in this circumstance has white linoleum tiles (similar to the kitchen in which I grew up in but immaculately white and clean). I drop a pencil; it falls on the floor, bouncing, making marks all over the floor with each bounce. I feel horrible for dropping the pencil, and I decide to kneel on the floor, wiping the pencil off.

Aftermath and Analysis of the Dream

Retrospectively, I have thought about a writing process a former design professor went through in order to organize her teaching philosophy. She shared this with me in 2000 in one of the many teacher-student dialogues we had. One exercise involved revisiting a handwriting exercise she'd done as an elementary student. A misplaced mark on a wide-lined sheet of paper unknowingly introduced visual language to her at an early age. Realizing her mistake, she tried to rub the mark away, only making it more obvious. What she saw at the time as a mistake and failed attempt to make something go away, she can now see as a "visual anomaly" that draws the viewer's attention to that spot first. For me, this was a lesson in perception, serendipity, and being willing to take risks in how one sees.

In the context of my life, this dream anticipates my move to New York and the anxiety surrounding it. A little more than two weeks before my move, at the time when I had this dream, I was overwhelmed by fears of regret. My life in Raleigh was more than comfortable. I had left a challenging and rewarding job as a high school art teacher. I had many friends. I was in a relationship with great potential. I was in a promising band. Things seemed like they could keep going with little effort; my life was on a sort of cruise control. The only thing lacking was my creative output. I hadn't painted all semester because of the draining nature of my job as a teacher. This absence of creative output was my primary reason for choosing to attend graduate school in New York.

When I revisited this dream a few weeks later in New York, I recognized its relevance to my former professor's teaching statement, about seeing the anxiety over a "mistake" as also a bold statement. Then I realized that these associations related to my anxiety and conflict about moving: Was it a mistake? Will I actually see it in time as a bold, life-changing statement? Will what I gain justify what I have given up? Can we ever know the full implications of our decisions in the moment when we make them?

This dream also dealt with my recollections of my parents' attitudes about success. By dropping the pencil on the floor, making marks, the floor looked like my adolescent family kitchen floor.

My mother with her compulsion to keep everything new and clean taught me at a very early age to take care of everything I owned. Now I also associate with this a message about risk-taking. Taking care of an object meant preserving its condition, even if that meant not using it to its fullest extent and thus hindering its original function. Taking care of what a person owns seemed for my mother a way to demonstrate responsibility and feel successful.

My father, a well-respected ichthyologist and college professor who died of cancer when I was twenty-two was, on the other hand, much more reckless and haphazard with objects. He seemed to use them to their fullest, being not as concerned with their longevity. I think of such things as the bumper of his pick-up truck rusting through because of hauling saltwater-soaked dive gear around for years. It's funny to remember how riding to elementary school with my father in that truck embarrassed my brother and me.

At some point, I think I may have unconsciously associated destroying the tools used to attain knowledge and understanding as a necessary part of the process of learning. In college, this led me to destroy many brushes and waste a lot of paint in my quest for understanding. A greater lesson for me may be the anxiety in, but the necessity for, making messes and dirtiness in the process of creativity and attaining success.

Helene Brandt, 68-year-old New York sculptor and former dancer

The Dreamer:

Helene has been artistically propelled all her life. Though exposed to art and music lessons as a child, early on she decided she really wanted to dance. At sixteen she took a part-time office job to pay for dance lessons and continued this exciting enterprise until she was twenty-six and had two children. At that point she decided that sculpture was what she wanted to devote her life to. Over the years this three-dimensional art has enriched her life as she has had to face such sad things as her mother's suicide and her first-born son's brain damage from meningitis. The way Helene's work has moved from cages to a bird on wheels is evidence of the vitality sculpture allows her to pursue and express

August 2004
Background and Preface to the Dream:

Growing up with a depressed artist mother and an extremely logical inventor father still influences my work. When I married at eighteen, I was determined to be a dancer, but despite enjoying the early training and experience, by age twenty-six I knew that visual art was what I wanted to devote my life to. With sculpture, not only was my whole body involved but even when I stopped, the art was still there. Soon I found myself using metal tubing to make cage sculptures that in 1980 I described as "about prisons, wombs, cages, city life, protection, and coercion. Everyone has a cage around them. It defines an inner identity. But if it becomes too dense, it shuts out other people." As I continued making cages, their lines gradually became more lyrical.

Then, in 2004: I had been working intensely for five months, six days a week, ten hours a day on the sculpture "Charion," a large, birdlike chariot made of twisted metal tubing. When I am working I become so lost in the process that I feel as if I am working for the evolving sculpture, not for myself. I have given over control. It is finished when it seems to exist entirely on its own and doesn't need me any more. What frightens me is the power of the object I have created. With "Clarion" and its wildly twisting tubes, I felt even more intimidated. How could someone like me make something like that? It's the conflict between me the artist and me the person who wants to pretend to be less capable than I am so people won't depend on me. I lose that other self when I'm working, but when the object is finished that self comes back to trouble me.

The Dream

I had to pick up a sculpture and decided to drive an old rusty truck about thirty feet long. I knew it would be hard to drive but I felt I could do it. I drove it to where the sculpture was. It was a relatively small and light structure. After I put the sculpture in the truck I realized I wasn't really able to handle the truck. It had been foolish of me to take it in the first place. I could never drive it to my studio in the crowded city and I better go back home. I had even more trouble driving it after that. I would enter an intersection carefully but with no confidence and was always afraid someone would crash into me. The home I drove to was the home of my childhood. I parked the truck across the street from our house and while walking up the front steps, looked back at the truck. It had become a horse-drawn truck and the horse was crossing the street and walking up the steps after me. At the top of the steps was a large puddle and the horse put its head into the water and began drinking furiously. I realized that I had forgotten to give the horse water and food for a long time and felt very bad. It could have died. I went into the house to look for a vessel in which I could bring some more water to the horse. I looked in closets and small rooms and realized in the dream that I was looking at places from different times in my life. I found only vessels that were too small or had circular openings in the bottom or were made of wire mesh. Then I decided to take a smallish white plastic basin, but I couldn't remember where the spigot was.

Aftermath and Analysis of the Dream

Thinking about the dream, I realized that the choice to take the truck wasn't rational since the sculpture I was to pick up is small and light. I was doing it only to prove to myself how powerful I can be, and I fail in the effort. So the dream is telling me that if I try to extend the power I have as an artist into my real life, I will do things that will put me in real danger. The home I drive to is the home of my childhood, the home of little Helene. During my psychotherapy I had done a series of "Therapy Cartoons" in which I sequentially drew nine frames, completing one after the other, not knowing how the story would develop. By the ninth frame came a revelation that was surprising but clarifying. Many of these dealt with the interactions of me as an adult artist and little Helene. She says I'm being arrogant to think I'm a real artist and feels I'm abandoning her. Through therapy this conflict had come out into the open. I'd also become more powerful as an artist and no longer had any doubts about being a "real" artist. But the intense experience of making "Charion" and the state I found myself in afterwards made me feel more vulnerable. In the dream, going back to the house of little Helene made me feel safer. I didn't have to go beyond where I was as an artist if I didn't want to. The horse now enters into the picture. It could mean that I didn't have to drive a large truck to go forward. I could use something more manageable like a horse. But in the dream I was conflicted about taking care of the horse. All the vessels I found didn't hold water and I couldn't remember how to fill them.

As a child, when my mother suffered deep depressions, I felt I had to perform the overwhelming task of taking care of her. This dream helped me to realize that being a person that people can depend on is not the same self-drowning task as trying to take care of my mother as a child. It also showed me that the fear still existed. After finishing "Charion" I wasn't sure what I wanted to do next. I thought I should retreat a bit and do something a little less wild. Now I know I'm going to continue to develop what I learned from working in a freer manner. After all the thoughts and feelings I had thinking about the dream, it is harder for me to retreat into something safer and more familiar.

Virginia Gibbons, 67-year-old NC sculptor and attorney

The Dreamer:

A lonely child with a physically at-risk younger brother, Virginia grew up in a small NC town and drew and painted from an early age. After earning an undergraduate degree in art history, she married and had two children. At age thirty-six, she went back to law school as a means of earning financial independence. She found sculpture and clay at age forty-four after not working at art for years. About that same time she separated from her husband. Her work is largely abstract but with discernible figurative references.

February 2004
Background and Preface to the Dream:

At the time of this dream, I had been making clay sculpture for almost twenty years. Yet my commitment to art had remained intermittent until I'd retired from the practice of law four years before. I had had some successes, but these were always followed by long periods of not working at all. Because of this and high expectations after retirement, continuing to struggle had left me uneasy. I had achieved some technical proficiency, but still felt that my work often lacked spirit or substance. Despite forcing myself to go to the studio on a regular basis I found little pleasure or satisfaction there. The feeling that I was wasting my time and kidding myself by thinking that I could make work that had any merit or significance haunted me.

Previous therapy and meditation practice had given me insight and relief from the chronic depression that had dogged me for years. Life outside the studio was generally good. I'd come to feel that my major demons were under control if not defeated.

The Dream

In my dream I am seeing through many eyes. This sensation is difficult to describe, but gives me a feeling of confidence and perspective. At the beginning of the dream I have a tiny, tiny baby—about 9 inches long. It is more like a toy than a real child. We are in a public place, perhaps a bus station. I know that I should feed him and I go into the rest room to prepare a bottle. I run hot water in the sink but worry that the sink is not clean. This makes me anxious, but I feel glad that I have not lost the baby or forgotten to feed him as I have in many previous dreams. In this dream I am aware of dreaming of a baby many times before. Again, seeing through many eyes, I keep going back to or discover the baby, and he is growing. I know that I should nurse the baby rather than try to bottle feed it, but I do not manage to do that. In the final scene of the dream I am lying on the ground. I massage my nipples and my breasts feel full and round. The sensation is pleasant and arousing. I know that I am ready to nurse the baby, but he is not with me on the ground. When I look up I see that there is a building close by and that people are looking at me from the windows. This makes me self-conscious but not ashamed. I think the building is a funeral home and the people inside are attending a memorial service. I go to find the baby and find him cozy in a big antique wooden bed. This is the first time that we have been together in a private space. I call out to him and he responds with a little chirp, the first sound I have ever heard him make. He looks healthy and has grown quite a lot. He stretches and I see that he has dark hair on his arms like I had as a child. I am very happy and satisfied that he is doing well and that I have cared for him in spite of everything. I have deep knowledge that both of us will be all right.

Aftermath and Analysis of the Dream

A few months before this dream, in the course of a workshop with Dr. Daniels, "Your Problems as the Source of Your Power," I had come face to face with the burning core of shame and alienation that I thought I'd left behind long before. This had led to a realization those feelings would probably always be with me because of my childhood. I'd grown up the misfit child in a dysfunctional family with an alcoholic parent. In the present, as I began to accept this part of me instead of trying to "fix" it, these feelings started to lose the power to control me. In fact, I suspect that the shame and alienation may, on some level, provide much of the impetus for my drive to find a voice through my work. For the first time I am giving myself permission to fail and paradoxically, this is the beginning of a new freedom in my work. I do not know that the work is better, but in a way that seems almost irrelevant. I do know that I am beginning to see it through my own eyes and not through those of some imagined other.

As I said, I have dreamed of the baby many times. This dream was substantially different. In past dreams I always realized with shock and guilt that I had forgotten or lost the baby. When I found it again, I was desperately afraid that I had neglected it for so long that it could not be saved. The feeling about this was similar to that of feeling the shame and alienation. In both, I felt flawed and afraid of being unable to cope, terrified of having others see my flaws and weaknesses. This dream was different because I felt confident throughout that I could care for the baby, and the dream ended with feelings of happiness and relief that the baby was thriving. Perhaps the baby is the part of me that I could not accept or even acknowledge before, that quivering core of secret shame. As I lay on the ground massaging my breasts, I was aware of the disapproving eyes of the people in the funeral home, but I was unashamed. I was also confident of my ability to nourish the baby with my own body. All the previous dreams had taken place in public places where there was a feeling of exposure and censure. This dream ended with the baby, healthy and growing, in a safe and private place.

This dream did not provide new knowledge but did provide the gut experience of what I had known conceptually. I actually experienced that feeling of nourishing myself and feeling strong and sure without more than passing concern for the opinions of others. I know there will always be struggles for me in this regard, but this dream has given me insight and encouragement.

Afterword

So, am I now a writer? With this, the fourth of five published books, how can that identity still be denied? The rational part of me recognizes this evidence and is factually convinced. The "under dog" still tries to deny this because of its wish to be loved by Father. But the greatest reward of my two-mirror dreaming and writing journey is that I no longer have to submit to my fantasy of wooden inadequacy in order to ward off Father's attacks and cling to his "love." Instead, since I now can recognize such debilitating feelings as defensive, I can push them aside so that I and my writing can show our power. This has made both writing and living wonderfully more gratifying. I will remain forever grateful to my writing and to my dreaming, and to Dr. H. for teaching me how to learn from them. I wish you and your creating similar freedom.

Appendix

(1) HOW TO EXECUTE YOUR TWO-MIRROR PROCESS

Steps you need to take to make use of the two-mirror process:

a. Write a detailed story line of your life complete with details of things/ feelings/issues dominant at different periods and with a detailed description of your current psychological situation.

b. Gradually develop the habit of appraising your work critically, striving to be honest and precise about its strengths and weaknesses. Also, remember that flaws recognized *can* be keys to freedom.

c. Develop the habit of recording your dreams as well as their dates.

d. Once the process has begun, continue it as follows:

Be Attentive Regarding Your Work

Observe and think about your work in detail—both the process of creating it and the product that results.

Record Your Dreams

Only after recording them, think about your dreams and then about how they relate to your work.

Continue This Process Over Time

Stay alert for the effects associated with growth and success as well as with failure. Remember to compare dreams with similar settings, problems or images, even when they occur years apart.

As you will see, this process is only as powerful as the individual pursuing it. The longer and harder you work, the greater your capacity will grow.

(2) DREAM TRUTHS TO REMEMBER

a. Stay on the lookout for new guises worn or new self-images in dreams and become more skilled at understanding their meanings.

b. Remember that "bad" dreams often serve the function of restoring the fear or low self-esteem one's unconscious is used to regarding as the "norm" and, therefore, required for stability.

c. Remember that a "good" dream may come as a "reward" for an actual failure to grow.

d. Remember that "anxiety dreams" serve the double function of reminding one that something in current life is anxiety provoking and allowing one to feel that all this distress is "just a dream."

e. Always ask "Why *this* dream at *this* time?"

f. Always respond to the place and time of a particular dream with the questions, "How was I feeling and/or what was I doing in that place/time?" or "What was happening to me then/there?"

Bibliography

Acocella, Joan. "Blocked." *The New Yorker*. June 14/21, 2004 issue.

Altman, L. *The Dream in Psychoanalysis*. International Universities Press, Inc., New York, 1969.

Arieti, Silvano. *Creativity—The Magic Synthesis*. Basic Books, Inc., New York, 1976.

Deri, Susan K. *Symbolization and Creativity*. International Universities Press, Inc., New York, 1984.

Erikson, Erik H. "The Dream Specimen of Psychoanalysis." *Journal of the American Psychoanalytic Association*. Vol. 2, 1954, pp. 5-56.

Federn, Paul. "Ego Feeling in Dreams." *Ego Psychology and the Psychoses*. Basic Books, Inc., New York, 1952.

Felstiner, Mary Lowenthal. *To Paint Her Life: Charlotte Salomon in the Nazi Era*. Harper Collins Publishers, New York, 1994.

Flaherty, Alice W. *The Midnight Disease*. Houghton Mifflin Co, Boston, 2004.

Flanders, Sara, (Ed.). *The Dream Discourse Today*. Routledge, New York and London, 1993.

Fosshage, James. "The Organizing Functions of Dream Mentation." *Contemporary Psychoanalysis*. Vol. 33, 1997, pp. 429-458.

French, Thomas, and Fromm, Erika. *Dream Interpretation: A New Approach*. Basic Books, New York, 1964.

Freud, Sigmund. *The Interpretation of Dreams*. The Modern Library, New York, 1900.

Gedo, John E. *Portraits of the Artist*. The Guilford Press, New York, 1983.

Gedo, John E. *The Artist and the Emotional World.* Columbia University Press, New York, 1996.

Greenberg, R., and Pearlman, C. "An Integrated Approach to Dream Theory: Contributions From Sleep Research and Clinical Practice." *The Functions of Dreaming.* Moffitt, A., Kramer, M. & Hoffman, R. (Eds.). State University of New York Press, New York, 1993, pp. 363-380.

Greenson, Ralph R. "The Exceptional Position of the Dream in Psychoanalytic Practice." *Explorations in Psychoanalysis.* International Universities Press, New York, 1978, pp. 387-414.

Hartmann, Ernest. "Nightmares and Boundaries in the Mind." *The Nightmare: The Psychology and Biology of Terrifying Dreams.* Basic Books, Inc., New York, 1984.

Kolodny, Susan. *The Captive Muse: On Creativity and Its Inhibition.* Psychosocial Press, Madison, Connecticut, 2000.

Kubie, Lawrence S. *Neurotic Distortion of the Creative Process.* University of Kansas Press, Lawrence, Kansas, 1958.

Kubie, Lawrence S. *Practical and Theoretical Aspects of Psychoanalysis.* International Universities Press, Inc., New York, 1950.

Lansky, Melvin R., (Ed.). *Essential Papers on Dreams.* New York University Press, New York, 1992.

Lippmann, Paul. *Nocturnes: On Listening to Dreams.* The Analytic Press, Hillsdale, NJ, 2000.

Mendelsohn, R. *The Manifest Dream and Its Use in Therapy.* Jason Aronson, New Jersey, 1990.

Milner, Marion. *On Not Being Able to Paint.* International Universities Press, Inc., New York, 1957.

Natterson, J. (Ed.). *The Dream in Clinical Practice.* Aronson, New York, 1980.

Palombo, S. *Dreaming and Memory: A New Information Processing Theory.* Basic Books, New York, 1978.

Pontalis, J.B. *Frontiers in Psychoanalysis: Between the Dream & Psychic Pain.* International Universities Press, Inc., New York, 1977.

Reiser, Morton. *Memory in Mind and Brain: What Dream Imagery Reveals.* Basic Books, Inc., New York, 1990.

Rose, Gilbert J. *The Power of Form—A Psychoanalytic Approach to Aesthetic Form.* International Universities Press, Inc., New York, 1980.

Rose, Gilbert J. *Trauma and Mastery in Life and Art.* Yale University Press, Inc., New Haven and London, 1987.

Rothenberg, Albert. *Creativity and Madness.* The Johns Hopkins University Press, Baltimore and London, 1990.

Segal, Hanna. "The Function of Dreams." *Do I Dare Disturb the Universe?* J.S. Grotstein (Ed.). Caeswa Press, Beverly Hills, California, 1981.

Sharpe, Ella. *Dream Analysis.* Hogarth Press, London, 1937.

Socarides, Charles W., and Kramer, Selma, (Eds.). *Work and Its Inhibition: Psychoanalytic Essays.* International Universities Press, Inc., Madison, Connecticut, 1996.

Solms, Mark. "New Findings on the Neurological Organization of Dreaming: Implications for Psychoanalysis." *Psychoanalytic Quarterly.* Vol. 64, 1995, pp. 43-67.

Solms, Mark. *The Neuropsychology of Dreams.* Lawrence Erlbaum Associates, Publishers, New Jersey, 1997.

Stolorow, Robert, and Atwood, George. "The Intersubjective Perspective." *Psychoanalytic Review.* Vol. 83, 1996, pp. 181-194.

Stolorow, Robert, and Atwood, George. "Psychoanalytic Phenomenology of the Dream." *Structures of Subjectivity.* The Analytic Press, Inc., New Jersey, 1984.

Vaillant, George E. *Adaptation to Life*. Little, Brown and Company, Boston, 1977.

Weiss, Joseph. "Dreams and Their Various Purposes." *The Psychoanalytic Process: Theory, Clinical Observation & Empirical Research*. Guilford Press, New York, 1986.

Winnicott, D.W. *Playing and Reality*. Tavistock Publications, London, 1971.

0-595-34393-7

Printed in the United States
28936LVS00005B/361-561